Divination with Osteomancy

A Beginner's Guide to Throwing the Bones

MONIQUE JOINER SIEDLAK

Oshun
Publications

Divination with Osteomancy: A Beginner's Guide to Throwing the Bones© Copyright 2021 by Monique Joiner Siedlak

ISBN: 978-1-956319-00-2

All rights reserved

The content contained within this book may not be reproduced, duplicated or transmitted without direct written permission from the author or the publisher.

Under no circumstances will any blame or legal responsibility be held against the publisher, or author, for any damages, reparation, or monetary loss due to the information contained within this book, either directly or indirectly.

Legal Notice

This book is copyright protected. It is only for personal use. You cannot amend, distribute, sell, use, quote or paraphrase any part, or the content within this book, without the consent of the author or publisher.

Disclaimer Notice

Please note the information contained within this document is for educational and entertainment purposes only. All effort has been executed to present accurate, up to date, reliable, complete information. No warranties of any kind are declared or implied. Readers acknowledge that the author is not engaged in the rendering of legal, financial, medical or professional advice. The content within this book has been derived from various sources. Please consult a licensed professional before attempting any techniques outlined in this book.

By reading this document, the reader agrees that under no circumstances is the author responsible for any losses, direct or indirect, that are incurred as a result of the use of the information contained within this document, including, but not limited to, errors, omissions, or inaccuracies.

Cover Design by MJS

Cover Image by Fotofabrika and ndefender @depositphotos.com

Published by Oshun Publications

www.oshunpublications.com

Books in the Series
_____

Divination Magic for Beginners

Divination with Runes: A Beginner's Guide to Rune Casting

Divination with Diloggún: A Beginner's Guide to Diloggún and Obi

Check out these titles!

SIGN UP TO THE NEWSLETTER
MAGICKAL CORRESPONDENCES
MONIQUE JOINER SIEDLAK
GET UPDATES, FREEBIES & GIVEAWAYS
mojosiedlak.com/magic-newsletter

Contents

Introduction	xi
1. Bone Casting History	1
2. Meaning Behind Throwing the Bones	15
3. What Is Used To Throw The Bones?	23
4. Collecting and Creating Your Own Bone Set	31
5. Preparing a Bone-Casting Set	39
6. Caring and Feeding Your Bones	53
7. Entering Into a Relationship with Your Bones	57
8. What Questions Are Best For Bone Readings?	65
9. Using Your Own Bone Set	73
Conclusion	89
References	91
About the Author	99
More Books by Monique	101
Last Chance	105
Thank You!	107

Introduction

Bone casting is one of the most ancient forms of divination in the world. It is used by a plethora of cultures from all around the globe for divination, spiritual and magical purposes. This book will delve you into the world of bones, exploring the many traditions and practices, including the Zulu sangomas of Southern Africa, to the Central Americas, to the Middle East.

Very little is known about the origins of the practice, mainly due to the nature of human archaeological remains. Archaeological sites are often filled with many different bones from various species collected during hunting, scavenging, and foraging over hundreds of years. It is difficult to determine whether the bones were waste products or kept for divination purposes. Some archaeological evidence does show that bones were often marked with significant notches, symbols, or colors, but these finds are rare. Much of the information we have today comes from oral traditions, and storytelling passed down from generation to generation.

Bone casting is classified as a form of divination, which includes any methods of seeking knowledge that uses supernatural means. Divination is one of many different forms of

Introduction

traditional healing, prayer, traditional medicines, sacrifices, witchcraft, and ancestral worship.

Though so many diverse cultures practice bone casting, it is strictly speaking a form of animism. Animism believes that everything possesses a soul or can be inhabited by spiritual energy and entities. The precise details will differ from culture to culture. Still, most view humans as equals to the rest of the natural world, including plants, animals, fungi, objects, places, climates, and the elements. In this worldview, people must attract the attention and favor of spirits by appeasing them. This is necessary to survive, as the spirits help locate and secure food, averting dangers, dealing with interpersonal rifts, and treating illnesses.

Bone casting is most prominent in Southern African cultures, where the belief in ancestors is prevalent. In this type of belief system, the ancestors are believed to have powers and abilities that allow them to intervene in the lives of mortal people on the surface of the Earth. The spirits are not a direct line of communication with God, but they are still revered as divine beings. Ancestors include family members that form part of a person's direct lineage. They can extend back to countless generations assuming the line remains unbroken. However, the animist worldview associated with ancestral worship also places great importance on the descendants of the ancestors, including the currently living people and those still to come.

Similar casting objects exist in other world regions, such as in Central America, where corn kernels are used instead of bones. The practices are based on much the same concepts. The ancestral spirits communicate through the objects to deliver important messages, advice, or warnings.

The divination practice is similar to other methods, such as scapulomancy. Scapula bones from the shoulders of sheep or goats are inscribed and burned to gain information.

This book will also look into the tools and materials

commonly used in bone casting practices, often accompanied by elaborate ceremonies and rituals. Numerous materials are used in bone casting, even among traditional healers such as Sangomas. Objects such as shells, coins, stones and crystals, amulets, and personal mementos can easily be incorporated into a bone casting set. There are also many different customs associated with the throwing surfaces used in bone casting, which will be discussed.

The process of obtaining bones can be difficult, dirty, and futile. In ancient times, people were more accustomed to dealing with the bodies of animals. People partook in hunting and butchering activities and were naturally familiar with the anatomy of various species. It was easy to collect bones of many different shapes and sizes from other animals. However, people in modern times are alienated from the process of food production. People, on average, do not grasp the processes involved with taking life and preparing meat for consumption. It is more difficult to source bones that have not been damaged during butchering. Luckily, there are still options available. Many divination practitioners have taken to the internet to spread their wealth of knowledge and insight. You can easily purchase bone casting sets of many different styles and qualities, which can be personalized and transformed into your magical tools. It is also possible to prepare your own bones if you are lucky enough to access an animal carcass. This book will guide you through cleaning and treating bones so that they look beautiful, adequately preserved, and can be used in divination practices.

Bones used for ceremonial purposes need to undergo specific rituals to make them clean and suitable for use. Spirits will not work with tainted or unclean objects unless those spirits themselves are tainted and impure. The ceremonial preparation of bones includes cleansing and blessing them. Cleansing refers to spiritual cleansing, as the bones will already be physically clean. Spiritual cleansing is an ancient and widespread practice associated with removing negative energy and entities from objects, spaces, and people. Blessing is another spiritual practice that involves infusing bones and other objects with good energy that you would actually want to work with. Hundreds of different methods are used to bless and cleanse magical objects, ranging from bathing them in the sun's light to burying them underground. Each of the various methods will serve a different purpose and remove or infuse a specific type of energy. Practitioners will need to be able to select and create their own cleansing and blessing rituals. This book will provide an excellent framework from which to work.

Building a connection with the bones and their animal spirits is a crucially important aspect of this divination practice. You will be introduced to the reasons for creating meaningful relationships with each of the bones and objects used in casting and methods that you can use and test to see which will work best for you and your practice.

Finally, we can begin to cast our bones. Understanding how to interact with the bones will improve the accuracy of your reading, and asking them the right kind of questions will lead to more productive castings. Unlike many other forms of divination, bones are suited to a wide range of questions and topics. They can be used to answer open-ended questions or provide short, concise answers. It all depends on how you phrase your question. Another important aspect is the methods you use to shake, mix, and randomize your bones before casting and the actual manner in which you cast bones. The book will explore some of the most common methods for casting, such as the left-hand method or the clockwise method. You will also be introduced to some of the methods used to read and interpret the bones.

This will serve you along your divination journey and help you become a more compassionate, caring, and well-connected spiritual practitioner. This is only a guide, and the world of divination is open and endless. You are always

Introduction

encouraged to do research and build your understanding and appreciation for history and forge your own path. Always remember that you are also a divine being, though you have not transcended yet. You, too, will enter the spirit world one day, and you can participate in the bone casting of your descendants. You experience the world in a way that is entirely different from anybody else. The accumulation of life experiences, knowledge, and skills results in a practitioner with valuable insights and opinions on any topic. Use this ability wisely and responsibly to improve your own life and the lives of your loved ones and your community. Use the spirit world to bring healing and peace, as well as unity and harmony.

ONE

Bone Casting History

THE HISTORY OF BONE CASTING IS A RICH AND DIVERSE TALE, being practiced by many different cultures across the globe. The exact origin of the practice is unknown but decidedly ancient. The prevalence of the tradition amongst many Southern African peoples lends credence to the hypothesis that the practice originates in these regions. Many different cultures, including the Zulu, Ndebele, Shona, and Chokwe, have variations of bone throwing traditions, especially the four-tablet tradition. Four-tablet divination uses four tablets, two male and two female tablets, each designated into binary groups such as junior or senior. For example, a tablet set will have a junior male tablet, a junior female table, a senior male tablet, and a senior female tablet. Casting the four tablets can result in 16 possible outcomes based on how the tablets fall about one another. The Zulu people of South Africa are amongst the most famous bone casting practitioners.

Zulu Sangomas

South Africa has a rich history of spiritual and divination practices. The traditional healers of the Zulu Nation are known as sangomas, referring to 'Ngoma,' which is a set of beliefs and spiritual practices relating to ancestral spirits. Sangomas undergo rigorous training. Along with initiations, their training covers topics such as divination, herbal medicine, channeling. Working with ancestral spirits, cleansing and blessing of magical objects, entering and facilitating trance-states using drumming and dancing, dream interpretation, learning the Zulu language, spiritual counseling, beadwork, and further education and training of new sangomas. Strictly speaking, sangomas can be split into two groups, sangomas who work with ancestral spirits and inyangas who work with the healing properties of plants and animals.

Sangomas partake in a type of bone casting that is also called sangoma. It is also practiced by neighboring people, including the Xhosa, Ndebele, and Swazi. Sangomas use bone casting to communicate with ancestral spirits, 'amadlozi,' to provide knowledge about future or unknown events or any messages that the spirits deem important. Bones are used but so too are objects like shells, stones, coins, and personal trinkets. This practice has also made its way to North America during the slave trade. The practice took root amongst disenfranchised African communities in the southern parts of the United States.

A sangoma will meet with their clients in special huts, where they sit across from the client and discuss their lives and the issues they face. The aim is to provide a holistic approach to healing, incorporating spiritual, emotional, physical, and mental health. The bones are shaken in a bag before blessing and consecrating them with smoke, herbs, and incantations. They are then cast down onto a flat surface covered by cloth or animal hide. The sangoma will then read the bones. Understanding how and where they land, which side is facing upwards, which bones are near to or touching each other, which bones fell further away and landed close by, where the bones are pointing, etc. The client will also impart their essence onto the bones by speaking a phrase, spitting, or blowing into the bones' bag. Interpreting the bones is a skill that must be practiced and developed over time, and sangomas train for many years before becoming practitioners.

"*My grandfather told me that a Sangoma must be able to draw knowledge from what he called 'the Hidden Lake.' He said a huge unseen lake somewhere in the spirit world where all the knowledge of the universe —past, present, and future—is to be found. You must never again say that you do not know something. You must just ask the lake, the unseen lake, to provide you with the knowledge that you seek...*" (Mutwa, 1999).

Vusamazulu Credo Mutwa

One of the most famous sangomas in modern history is Mutwa. He was born in Zululand, now known as KwaZulu-Natal, on the East coast of South Africa in 1921. During this time, South Africa was deeply entrenched in political and cultural battles. The British and Dutch colonists worked to alienate and segregate the indigenous peoples, including the Zulus. Mutwa's parents shared many of these struggles, with his mother being a Christian and his father following the traditional beliefs of the Zulu kingdom. His parents could not reconcile the differences since the British imposed Christianity on the people and attempted to erase their cultural heritage.

Mutwa moved around a lot during his early years, traveling between his father and mother's family homesteads. A group of mineworkers violently beat Mutwa during his teenage years, marking the beginning of his spiritual journey. Mutwa found that western medicine could not help him recover from his injuries and trauma. So he began investigating his traditional heritage and sought aid from traditional healers in his mother's village. This experience would stay with him forever; Mutwa turned his back on Christian belief systems and chose to embrace his African roots fully.

He began training to become a sangoma. Mutwa spent many years traveling around South Africa and Swaziland, working with traditional healers and catholic priests. He spoke with many people, listened to their experiences, and heard their stories. This helped to develop a comprehensive knowledge base.

Mutwa made many prophecies and predictions. Such as the events of September 11th, the assassination of political activist Chris Hani, and the firing of acting South African president Thabo Mbeki and many others that have come to pass.

One of the most significant contributions made by Mutwa was in his efforts to protect and conserve South African cultural heritage. He could see the effects of western colonialism on the indigenous people and feared the loss of diverse cultures. In this way, many of his detractors claimed that Mutwa was an apartheid apologist, supporting segregation policies. However, Mutwa supporters claim he only promoted the autonomy of different tribes and cultures to govern themselves without outside interference.

In 1947, Mutwa began setting up the Kwa-Khaya Lendaba cultural village to showcase the wide variety of cultures, practices, and belief systems in South Africa. He used his artistic abilities to create models representing different building styles and installed African folklore and mythology characters. Within these villages, people worked in traditional activities like beadwork or weaving to educate Westerners and African people about the rich cultural heritage. He showed people that African history is much more extensive than the arrival of the Dutch in South Africa. It should be celebrated and publicized, not practiced in secrecy.

"Don't get angry over shadows. Let the pains of the past go by because if you do, your soul becomes corrupted; your soul becomes warped." --Mutwa

Chokwe Tahis

In Central and Southern Africa, the Chokwe people have traditional healers known as tahi, who undergo similar training to the Zulu sangomas. In this tradition, the tahi uses bone casting to communicate with the spirits known as 'hamba,' who possess people and interfere with their lives. The Tahi use bone casting to communicate with these spirits and drive them away. Bones, shells, stones, coins, and other small objects are placed into a divination basket, called a 'ngombo ya kusekula.' The basket is made from sacred plants and is woven, coiled, or spun in unique and sacred ways. There are often decorations such as bells, animal skins, furs, teeth, and shells adorned on the outside of the basket, and markings of white and red clay. All of the pieces contribute to the spiritual power of the divination basket.

When carrying out a bone-casting ceremony, a tahi will shake the bones and objects inside the 'ngombo ya kusekula.' The action is compared to winnowing, where grains are shaken to remove their husks. In the same way, the bones are shaken to remove any negative energy or spirit or separate the falsehood from the truth. The tahi are often possessed when shaking the divination baskets, as ancestral spirits enter their bodies and guide their hands. Unlike other methods, the bones are not cast onto a surface but kept inside the divination basket. The location of the bones to the red and white clays are among the essential features. The bones will reveal personal problems, which the tahi and their client will discuss. A final step in this practice is where the client will take a piece of bone away with them as an amulet. The amulet will serve to protect the client from possession by malicious spirits, help them channel energy from ancestral spirits, and keep them on a healing path.

Tswana Ngwaketse

The Tswana people of Botswana and surrounding regions employ a form of bone casting divination known as Ngwaketse. Carried out by a spiritual practitioner called 'ngaka.' An ngwaketse bone-set comprises four principal bones and several accessory bones. However, they can include materials other than bone, such as shells, seeds, or stones. The prominent bones relate to people seeking out divination, and the accessory bones about different aspects of society. Each bone has a specific name and gender, which the practitioner uses to interpret the pattern.

People will refer to the bones when making important decisions or getting help with a crisis in their lives. The practitioner will consult with their client to determine why they choose to use bone casting and the problems they're facing. The bones are cast onto a flat surface and interpreted. The four principal bones are the most important and offer insight into the person's life. The practitioner will look at how the bones fall and interact with one another to identify different aspects of the person's life that can be improved or aspects that need to be removed. Considerable importance is placed on the community. An individual's well-being is a function of the community as a whole and its interactions. This type of divination is not wholly concerned with the personal life of a single person. Instead, it focuses on their place within the larger community.

Shona Traditions

The Shona people of Zimbabwe hold a belief system centered around the god known as Mwari. Within this belief system, mortal humans are deemed unworthy of communicating directly with Mwari. So they use ancestral spirits as intermediaries. Spiritual healers and divination practitioners are almost always women, with men dealing with other issues like politics, warfare, and farming.

Spiritual practitioners use four-tablet divination. Using four specially crafted tablets called 'Hakata,' which can be made from bone, wood, stone, ivory, or horn. Each tablet has a name and assigned meaning, being decorated with intricate symbolic meanings. A zigzag border is commonly used to mark the front surface of the tablets. Two of the tablets are junior tablets, while the other two are senior tablets. The junior and senior tablets are further designated into males and females. The junior tablets are marked with notches at the bottom: the male tablet is marked with a single notch. It is called 'Lumwe,' while the female tablet is marked with two notches and is called 'Ntakwala.' The senior tablets do not have notches but pictures carved or inscribed into the surface. The senior male tablet is marked with a picture of an ax, spear, or some weapon and is called 'Chilume,' while the senior female tablet is marked with a house or an eye and is called 'Kwame.'

The tablets are cast onto a flat surface where they form a pattern that is then read and interpreted by the practitioner. A session can involve between 20 and 40 throws. The practitioner plays a significant role in influencing how the tablets fall based on how they are shaken and cast. The tablets can fall face up or face down. There are 16 possible outcomes based on the configuration of the face-up and face-down tablets. Each of the outcomes has a name and a meaning which are known to the practitioner.

Yoruba Obi

The Yoruba people of Nigeria, Togo, and Benin follow a belief system in which God manifests as various avatars on Earth called Orishas. The prophet Orunmila, who founded the religion, is one of the Orisha. He plays a role in revealing divinity and prophecy to the world. The divination aspects of the Yoruba religion are called Ifá. The Yoruba people use kola nuts, a palm nut, from the indigenous kola tree in divination work. These nuts, called 'Obi' in the Yoruba language, are used similarly to the bones of other belief systems, where they are shaken and cast to reveal messages from divine spirits. There are many types of Obi with different numbers of lobes; some are used for eating or as offerings. Similar to the Shona tradition, the four-lobed Obi are used in rituals and ifá ceremonies. A divination board called 'opon ifá' is used to contain the Obi.

Ifá practitioners are called Babalawos (male) or Iyanifás (female), they use Obi to communicate with their Orisha before making important personal or collective decisions. Fresh obi nuts are used each time instead of using the same set of bones. The Babalawo or Iyanifá will cleanse the Obi before opening it up and separating the four segments. They will hold two parts in each hand before appealing to the Orisha and then casting them onto the ground.

The Obi is interpreted based on how the segments fall: up or down. The positions correlate to a symbol from the sixteen principal Odu Ifá, a sacred Yoruban text. The Odu Ifá comprises sixteen parts. Each with sixteen possible interpretations, making up 256 possible outcomes. These outcomes relate to different aspects of life. For example, if all four nuts land upwards, this relates to the 'Eji Ogbe,' a symbol of plenty. If the first two nuts land downwards, and the last two land upwards, this relates to the 'Owonrin meji,' a symbol of victory. If all the nuts land downwards except the second nut, this relates to the 'Ika Meji,' which symbolizes longevity. The practitioner will ask one question and then cast the nuts, interpreting the answer and then moving on to another question and recasting.

"He who brings the kola nut brings life." –Yoruba Proverb

Central America Corn Casting

A practice used throughout Central America, originating in the Aztec civilization, is the casting of corn kernels to predict the future. Divination was an integral part of daily life in the Aztec kingdoms with significant events and decisions preceded by a form of prophecy or fortune-telling. Much of Mesoamerica was heavily reliant upon the maize plant, which had been cultivated in the region over hundreds of years. The planting, growing, and harvesting of corn was considered akin to birth, life, and death. It is still a commonly used practice amongst many different people, using corn and other casting methods.

Dried kernels are used, which have been specially grown, harvested, dried, and prepared for use in kernel casting. Some rituals may call for less than five kernels while others use more than 100; the number dramatically varies. Each kernel has a top and bottom side, as well as a front and backside. The kernels are cast into a flat surface covered by a white cloth or into a water basin. The edges of the cloth or the basin can also have meanings, such as cardinal directions. The positioning of the kernels in relation to each other is a key factor.

For example, corn kernels are often used to assess and deal with marital problems. When kernels are cast, one will be assigned to each partner. If they fall near each other and point in the same direction, this is a good sign that they are on the same page. However, if the kernels fall far apart from each other, or if they point in the wrong directions, this is a bad sign. Other nearby kernels may indicate infidelity, or conversely, a supportive network of friends and family. If a kernel falls with the flat face upwards, this is a negative sign. However, if the concave side faces upwards, this is a positive sign. The kernels are interpreted in this way to help people with their daily problem.

Casting Lots

Casting lots, also known as cleromancy, is a practice that appears to have originated in Ancient Rome but is popularized in modern times through the Bible and the Torah. This practice would have been prevalent in the ancient streets and villages of the Middle and Near East, similar to modern-day dice-rolling or coin-flipping. The practice is rarely used for divination purposes. The religious texts have explicit warnings against prophets, fortune-tellers, diviners, and sorcerers. Instead, lots are cast as a game or to determine random outcomes using luck or chance. Lots can be made of bones, but more common materials include stones, sticks, dice, or coins. Meaning is assigned to the different objects making up the lot like the different sides of a dice. For example, the Bible tells of casting lots to determine how to divide up a piece of land amongst a group of farmers. Similarly, ancient priests used to cast lots to assign temple jobs randomly. Many were cast to find a replacement for Judas Iscariot's disciple after he betrayed him in the famous biblical account.

Knucklebones

The use of knucklebones from a sheep or a goat is a common occurrence in many regions worldwide. The ancient Greeks were known to play games using these uniquely shaped bones. However, the tradition has continued across most of Asia, parts of America and Austronesia, Europe, and North Africa. Knucklebones come from the talus bone in the ankle joint of hooved animals such as goats, sheep, and deer.

Knucklebones are used in divination practices in central Asia, eastern Europe, Mongolia, China, and many other cultures. For example, in Mongolia, the bones are called 'shagai,' and each side is named; horse, goat, sheep, and camel. Two of the sides, horse and sheep, are convex in shape; the

Divination with Osteomancy

other two sides are concave, but all are discernible from one another. A set comprises four knucklebones. It is not uncommon to find markings on the different sides to help identification. However, many knucklebone sets are decorated richly with paints, images, and markings.

Knucklebones are cast in the same way as dice, four at a time. They are used to answer a series of yes or no questions. The horse and sheep sides of the shagai are good luck, while the goat and camel are bad luck. The orientation of the individual dice is noted. Still, the configuration of all four shagai is the primary concern, in much the same way as the four-tablet system seen in Africa. Each of the possible castings of the four knucklebones is assigned a meaning. For example, casting four horses is the most potent symbol of good luck. However, if you cast one sheep and three goats, this is terrible luck. Most meanings denote a degree of success or difficulty in carrying out a task.

Chinese Oracle Bones

Oracle bones were a divination tool used by diviners in China during the Shang Dynasty. Though oracle bones are not used in bone casting rituals, the practice is still worth mentioning. Oracle bones were used to predict the future or foretell fortunes or bad luck. Priests mainly used the method for the Shang kings. Before being blessed and inscribed with a question, the bones were removed from the body of a slaughtered animal and cleaned and scraped of flesh. The questions were generally directed at ancestors following the belief system of the time. The ancestors would guide the oracle bones on various topics, including the effectiveness of their rituals and ceremonies, health concerns, crop and weather issues, or interpersonal problems. These inscriptions can still be seen on Chinese artifacts and serve as the basis of the modern Chinese language script. The question would be spoken out loud as an incantation before burning the bone.

Oracle bones were burned using a hot rod or piece of coal. Scapula bones have a natural bowl shape, in which the rods or coal would be placed. This would cause the bones to crack. The bones were often broken multiple times in succession, with each crack being noted and interpreted. Sometimes small holes were drilled into the surface before burning the bone, and the hot rods were placed through these holes. Their placement would undoubtedly affect the cracking, and the diviner would strategically select the order of the holes. The exact meanings of different crack shapes and arrangements are unfortunately not well known.

Using scapulas for divination purposes is called scapulimancy, and the use of burned materials is called pyromancy. However, this tradition evolved to using an increasing number of tortoise shells, or plastrons, instead of scapulae. The tortoise shells were used in the same way, using inscriptions and then placing a hot object into the middle like a bowl until it cracked.

Nordic Runes

Runes are symbolic characters or letters from the Germanic alphabet. However, a similar version also existed in the Scandinavian languages. Popularized by the Nordic Vikings, called the 'Futhark.' Runes were used in many ways, including keeping records, writing down important information, and inscribing carvings, statues, and amulets. The symbols were believed to hold great power and wisdom, granting the wielder the ability to shape the world around them and change fate. One of the primary Nordic texts, the Poetic Edda, contains a verse called the Sigrdrífumál—which mentions signs that include magical charms, healing signs, and spells full of goodness and gladness.

Divination with Osteomancy

However, one of the most famous tales in Norse mythology tells of Odin's trials and tribulations to gain the runes. In this story, the runes are a magical tool used by divine creatures to shape and determine fate. Odin desired the power of the runes, but the runes will only reveal themselves to those who are worthy. Odin proceeded to hang himself from the branch of the great Tree of Life, 'Yggdrasil.' He stabbed himself with a spear before spending nine days and nights peering into the waters that were home to the runes. Eventually, the runes did reveal themselves to Odin and granted him their powers and wisdom through his sacrifice.

There are 24 runic characters, and each has a name and meaning assigned to it. For example, 'ansuz' means god and has the symbol ᚠ, 'mannaz' means man and has the symbol ᛗ, and 'fehu,' which means cattle with the ᚹ character. Runes are used in divination, fortune-telling and prophecy, and spells or curses. Rune sets are collections of bones, stones, seeds, or similar objects, with a rune inscribed onto each one.

Though not strictly a method of bone casting, the action of casting objects and reading them based on how they fall is comparable. Runes are traditionally stored in a bag and tossed onto a flat white surface to protect the runes from spiritual contamination. A person would consult the runes by grabbing hold of the runes within the bag, usually a predefined number such as three or four, based on the type of questions they ask. Keeping the question in mind, the person will cast the runes onto the surface to land in a pattern, each facing up or face down. The runes can then be read based on their positioning and configuration.

Scottish Speal Bones

Scottish speal bones were used in divination practices in very much the same way as Chinese oracle bones. The scapula of an animal, usually a goat or a sheep, was used to predict the future in a process called 'slinneanachd.' The animal would be butchered into different cuts and eaten following special rituals. In these rituals, it is forbidden to touch the bones with tooth or nail while eating, disrupting the naturally occurring markings. After properly cleaning and preparing the bone following formal procedures, the marks on the surface were read and interpreted by a diviner. There is very little information about this practice, primarily due to the strong oral tradition of these cultures, which chose not to write down their traditions. Most of the available information comes from second-hand accounts rather than primary sources.

More common applications using bones included the construction of amulets or charms made from bones. However, the Scottish people used human bones to curse people. They would remove bones from corpses that had been buried, awakening their souls and making them restless. The person in possession of the bones had command of the soul, and they could make it do their bidding by haunting others. A great fear was that the soul would take revenge on the person if they did not return the bones to the grave timeously.

"A strange habit of these Flemings is that they boil the right shoulderblade of rams but not roast them. Strip off all the meat and, by examining them, foretell the future and reveal the secrets of events long past. Using these shoulder blades, they have the extraordinary power of the divine what is happening far away at this very moment. By looking carefully at the little indents and protuberances, they prophesy with complete confidence periods of peace and outbreaks of war, murders, and conflagrations, the infidelities of married people, and the welfare of the reigning king, especially his life and death." –Gerald of Wales, in Journey Through Wales (1188).

TWO

Meaning Behind Throwing the Bones

What Is Bone Casting?

BONE THROWING IS A WITCHCRAFT PRACTICE STRONGLY associated with a belief in ancestors and their ability to influence events and animism, the idea that objects can contain spiritual energy. It is one of the most ancient and archaic forms of divination. Many practitioners and diviners come from long lineages that have carried out bone casting practices for hundreds of years. Bone casting predicts the future or makes prophecies and gains insight into personal or community problems.

The methods used to cast bones vary based on the practitioner's belief system and their followers. Bone casting is perhaps most prevalent in South Africa, where there is a strong culture of ancestor worship. The ancestors are believed to exist in the spirit world, exerting influence over the day-to-day lives of their descendants. Ancestors can be swayed with offerings and sacrifices, but they can also be angered by foolishness. Bones are used as a tool of communication with the spirit world because they are objects of death.

Bones come from the bodies of once-living beings that were born, lived, and died. They represent an integral connection to the cycle of life on earth. They hold the essence of the animal from which they came, and they can be used to communicate with the spirit world. Any natural products will contain the essence of nature. However, the process of obtaining bones from an animal makes them even more special. Traditionally, animals are hunted to feed one's family, village, or local community. Hunting cultures place great value and honor on the act of taking life with good reason, and the prey animals are revered. Tracking, hunting, and killing an animal is a sacred rite that human beings have been initiated into since Neolithic times. The process of butchering, cooking, and eating the animal is similarly essential. Respect must be offered to the animal's spirit. Many cultures give thanks to the animals that had their lives sacrificed for people to survive. In this way, bones possess the memory of the animals waking life and the process of being hunted. They contain the essence of the animal's spirit. Because they possess spiritual energy, they can also channel other spirits, such as one's ancestors. This is one way in which bone casting works.

There are many diverse sets of beliefs surrounding the spirits of animals. In some religions, animals are believed to be the reincarnated souls of deceased people. In other religions, animals are manifestations of divine beings, avatars of god on earth. This strong element of animism is crucial for bone casting. Diviners need to understand the animal from which their bones come. They must understand the natural hierarchy that animals live under, the role that the animal plays in their ecosystem, the behavior of the animal towards predators, competitors, and kin, and how they reproduce and die. All of these factors will play a role in the magic of the bones.

For example, a set of bones from a rat will have different features to the bones of a lion. In some cultures, rats are viewed as luck, fortune, or fertility symbols thanks to their highly opportunistic behaviors and high reproductive success rates. Compare this to the symbolism of a lion, which often represents supreme dominance and strength. The bones from each of these animals will provide different messages to the diviner.

What Is Divination?

The word divination means to 'be inspired by God' or gain insight using divine methods, rituals, or practices. Divination encompasses an exceedingly wide array of techniques used to foretell the future, make predictions or prophecies, communicate with the dead or ancestors, or ward harmful spirits or demons. Since antiquity, divination practices have been in use. Many of the oldest stories and tales mention the work of prophets or oracles that can control or predict the future.

The concept of divination is based on various belief systems in which divine beings choose to communicate with humans. This feature is not present in all belief systems. Many cultures worldwide reject the idea that divine beings would want to or have the capacity to communicate with mortal beings on earth. In some systems, such as the Zulu belief system, ancestral spirits serve as intermediaries between the divine beings and the people, allowing communication to occur. However, there are also belief systems in which direct communication with divinity is an accepted phenomenon.

Anthropologists describe two different forms of divination practices. Inductive and intuitive. Inductive divination involves extracting and interpreting meaning from objects. In contrast, intuitive divination involves the direct receiving of messages from the spirit world. These types of divination reflect fundamental differences in the underlying belief systems and worldviews. For example, two different belief systems can have drastically different ideas about the nature of reality, the nature of God, the nature of man, the purpose of man, the basis of morality, and the origin of the universe, life, and death.

A belief system that uses inductive divination will generally hold a worldview in which divine beings do not directly influence reality. Instead, the nature of reality is pre-planned and tends to organize itself according to this plan. Astrology is an excellent example of such a belief system in which gods do not directly control the movement of stars and planets. Instead, the movement of stars and planets is a part of a predefined plan. The movements and configurations of the planets are interpreted to infer messages from the gods. Inductive divination can be used to interpret how the leaves fall from a tree, the patterns on an animal's fur, or the pitch of a baby's cry.

Compare this to a belief system where it is believed that gods do communicate directly with men and influence reality. This belief system would use intuitive divination, receiving messages through trances or in dreams or prayers, speaking directly with a divine presence, and believing that the gods will affect the world. This belief system assumes that the human mind can engage directly with the spirit world or divine powers. For example, prayer is employed in countless religions, used as a tool of direct communication with God.

Intuitive and inductive divination are not mutually exclusive, and there is room for overlap. Interpretive divination includes any techniques implemented to bridge the gap between intuitive and inductive methods. For example, in bone casting, a sangoma will shake the bones. This is a type of intuitive divination, where the sangoma must decide how rigorously to shake and when the contents have been mixed enough. The process of casting the bones is inductive divination, as the sangoma must accept the configuration and patterns formed. The sangoma must then use their knowledge to identify, interpret and select the most relevant elements of the casting. This is interpretive divination.

Osteomancy and Pyromancy

There are hundreds of different divination techniques used worldwide. Osteomancy includes any practices that use bones. Bone casting is perhaps the most popular and well-known form of osteomancy, though scapulas are another common practice. Pyromancy consists of any practices that use fire, such as hot rods, to crack oracle bones. There are many different types of pyromancy, including the reading of shapes and figures in flames, the burning of herbs or the innards of animals, to the burning of tortoise shells. Below are some other forms of divination. Some may be familiar to you, but others may be new:

Acultomancy is the practice of reading and interpreting how needles fall onto a surface and their patterns.

Amniomancy is the practice of observing the color and consistency of the placenta after birth to predict the child's future.

Astrology involves using the movements of celestial bodies to make predictions about world events and personal issues.

Bibliomancy uses a random page from a book, often the bible, to predict future events based on the text.

Carromancy involves interpreting the patterns and shapes formed by melting wax.

Cartomancy is the practice of using playing cards to provide guidance or counseling by assigning meanings to different numbers, suits, and hands.

Dōbutsu uranai are Japanese animal horoscopes used to categorize people into groups with other characteristics based on their birth year.

Demonomancy involves the use of demons as a conduit for communication with the spirit world.

Electromancy is the practice of interpreting lightning strikes and electrical activity.

Fractomancy consists of interpreting the repeating geometric patterns known as fractals that form through many natural processes.

Gematria is a practice that uses the Hebrew Alphabet to decipher hidden messages in numbers, names, words, or phrases.

Hakata is a Shona bone-throwing practice with a four-tablet system.

Ifá is a Yoruba tradition using the four-lobed obi nuts.

Isopsephy is the practice of adding up the number value of letters in a phrase or word to expose hidden messages.

Kabbalah is an ancient school of Hebrew occultism and mysticism that uses codes and ciphers.

Lithomancy involves interpreting meaning from precious gems or stones.

Logarithmancy is the practice of using logarithms to elucidate answers or predict the future.

Mahjong is an oracle card game that can also be used as a fortune-telling device, similar to playing cards.

Meteromancy is the reading and interpreting meteor impacts and showers as signs from God.

Necromancy is the practice of communicating with the dead.

Oomancy involves the use of eggs to remove negative energy or make prophecies.

Palmistry is reading the lines on a person's palm to infer information about their past and future.

Plastromancy involves using the plastron from a tortoise or turtle to receive divine messages.

Scrying is a method of using reflective surfaces to detect or receive messages from the spirit world.

Shufflemancy is a modern method of divination relying on the shuffle algorithm of a music player to pass on messages from spirits or entities.

Turifumy involves reading into the shapes and patterns produced by smoke to infer meaning.

THREE

What Is Used To Throw The Bones?

Many different magical tools are used in bone casting practices around the world. The practice originated in ancient times when people did not have access to an abundance of raw materials. Most of their everyday products would be crafted from waste products accrued during hunting, foraging, and farming activities. Animal bones would have been a common occurrence in all homes as most people were responsible for sourcing and processing their food. Bones that are not eaten would be used in construction activities to help build tools or homes. Bones were commonly used to make hammers, buttons, needles, and weapons. However, waste was also common, resulting in excess bones.

The use of bones in bone casting is an integral element of the practice due to the nature of bones, which come from a living animal. They hold unique magical and spiritual properties that cannot be replicated in other items. However, this does not mean that non-bone materials are useless, as other objects will still hold spiritual energy. An example is the kola nuts, or Obi, used in the Yoruba traditions.

A bone throwing set can be made up of a single type of

bone or many bones, coming from a single animal or many animals. It can also include any variety of small objects, including other animal products such as teeth, claws, shells or feathers, shells, nuts, seeds, stones, gems, coins, keys, bottle caps, or dice. There are no rules or requirements for compiling your own set of objects for bone throwing. The only recommendations are to ensure that each object is assigned a relevant meaning and that the objects are small enough to handle.

It is not a requirement to use real bones, or any genuine animal products, in your practice. Practitioners are always encouraged to interact with the world in the most humane way possible. To many people, sourcing bones from animals is not considered humane. This is up to personal preference. A bone-casting set that contains no bones but instead many small trinkets and other natural objects will be just as valuable and effective. The applications will differ. For example, certain traditional and cultural practices will bar you from participating if you do not use specific tools such as natural bone. Most of these cultural practices are closed to newcomers regardless of their tools. They are exclusively practiced by people from long lineages and bloodlines.

Some Anatomy Lessons

Working with bones is an excellent way to learn more about the anatomy of humans and animals. You will very quickly and easily pick up on the names. The skeleton is a support structure that allows animals to move around. Muscles and tendons attach directly to the muscles and move them about. Bones are made from calcium and a network of proteins like collagen. In the center of a bone is the marrow cavity, where white blood cells are produced.

All vertebrates have a skeleton on the inside. Insects, on the other hand, have skeletons on the outside called exoskeletons. We will not discuss exoskeletons in this book. All in all, animals have the same basic layout. They have a skull attached to a spinal column. Limbs extend out from the spinal column and connect at the hip or shoulder joints. The internal organs are encased in rib bones.

There are four different bones: long bones, short bones, flat bones, and irregular bones. Long bones are, quite simply, bones that are long. This includes the bones of your legs, the femur, tibia and fibula, your arms, the humerus, radius, and ulna. Long bones also include the bones in your hands and fingers, called phalanges. Short bones are those that have similar lengths and widths; they are found in wrists, ankles, and knee joints. The knucklebones mentioned in a previous section are an excellent example of short bones. Flat bones have large, flat surfaces such as your skull and facial bones, the scapula, and ribs. Ribs are included with flat bones and not long bones because they have flat faces, whereas long bones are mostly round. Finally, irregular bones are oddly shaped, such as the hips or the vertebrae in the spine.

In some types of animals, the limbs have evolved to look a bit different. You can see this in hooved animals or animals with fins. In hooved animals, the limb is more like a finger than an arm, and the hoof itself is like a toenail. The names of these bones will be different.

Meaning

Each piece in your bone casting set must have its own meaning. You will need to account for various possible questions or issues wanting to be answered through the bones, such as family issues, money issues, health problems, etc. This will be a highly personalized process, and your set of bones will be unique.

Here are some questions to consider when compiling a bone casting set and assigning meanings to your objects. However, there are many more questions you could ask:

Which piece in the collection will represent the self?

How will you represent health, and what aspects of health are important to you?

Do you suffer from particular health issues that could be represented with an object separate from general health?

Which pieces will represent wealth, financial security, or fortune?

Which elements will represent family?

Do you need individual pieces for each person in your family, just one piece for the whole family unit, or both?

How do you want to represent love?

Do you need a piece for a love interest or your own heart?

Which elements will represent magic and the spirit world?

Which spirits are essential to you?

Which practices do you follow, and what kind of worldview do you hold?

Which pieces can be used to represent 'yes' and 'no' for binary questions?

Would you prefer one object for 'yes' and another for 'no,' or would you pick a double-sided object?

How will you represent negative aspects, such as bad intentions, ill-health or spiritual failings?

Which pieces will represent fertility, children, and youth?

How will you represent numbers?

Do you need objects that infer few or many?

Do you need objects that represent specific numbers or symbols?

Which pieces will represent binary choices, such as masculine and feminine, or light and dark, yes and no, up and down?

Ascribing Meaning

Now that you have a better idea of the different aspects of life that a bone-casting set would be concerned with, you can begin identifying pieces for each important meaning. Below are examples of the assigned meanings assigned to objects in a bone-casting set. keep in mind that there are no set definitions for any bone or object, and everything is open to changes and interpretation:

A mouse skull represents the self. A skull serves to house the brain, which is where the 'self' is manifested. Skulls can also represent intelligence, sentience, and thought.

A chicken wishbone represents luck, good fortune, and prosperity.

A claw represents anger, rage, or survival instinct.

A coin is used to represent yes or no answers.

A feather represents travel, flight, and the essence of freedom.

A femur bone represents the passage of time, growth, development, and aging.

A fossilized fish represents the past, the ancestors, and the passage of time.

A key can be used to represent the opening of doors, transitions, crossroads, and decision-making.

Amethyst crystal represents the spirit world, the soul, and the afterlife.

A penis bone represents virility and fertility.

A rib bone represents safety and security. Ribs are used to contain and protect the internal organs from harm.

Black stones represent evil or bad luck.

Knucklebone represents financial issues. The four sides of a knucklebone can hold different meanings, such as good fortune or debt, incoming money, or borrowers.

Quartz crystals represent protective energy and protective forces.

Sunflower seeds represent virility and growth.

Vertebrae and tail bones represent family members and loved ones.

White shells represent purification and the ocean.

White stones represent innocence and pure intentions.

The specific meanings behind each of the objects in a bone-casting set are often very personal and need not be shared with anybody. Diviners that use bone-casting will usually have a specially designated set used in consultation with clients, different from their own personal bone-throwing set.

Throwing Surface Coverings

Many different types of surface coverings are suitable for bone-casting. It is uncustomary to cast directly onto the ground unless special accommodations have been made. It is traditional in many cultures to cast into a white cloth. The cloth protects the bones from physical damage that can occur when casting. Still, it also protects the bones from spiritual influences by creating a barrier between the earth. The white color is viewed as a symbol of purity almost universally. It is used to maintain the objects' pure intentions and magical properties in the bone casting set.

Throwing surfaces can also be richly decorated or inscribed with symbols. Coverings can be made from other materials, including animal hide and animal furs, wooden boards and planks, or stone. In modern times, plastic alternatives are popular and can be created in many different shapes, patterns, and colors.

Layouts

There are many different layouts that you can use on your casting surface. A typical pattern is to split the cloth up into four quadrants, representing the cardinal direction points; north, south, east, and west. Instead of cardinal points, you can also use the classical elements—fire, earth, water, and air —with each element designated to a corner of the covering. In some traditions, the classical elements are tied to a particular cardinal direction, such as associating the fire element with the south. However, there are no steadfast rules, and the arrangement of elements differs across cultures and regions.

It is also not uncommon to see different covering

sections marked for various purposes, such as having a corner for 'yes' and 'no' questions and another corner with letters or numbers. This is comparable to the layout of an ouija board. Concentric circles are also used in bone-casting, with inner circles representing the self and your personal life. As you move outwards and the circles become more significant, they represent larger aspects of your life, such as friends and family. The community and the spirit world. The circles can also be used to express direct and indirect influences in your life. Past, present, and future layouts are also prevalent, with the covering being split into three sections.

Other Tools

Bags

Some other essential tools used in bone-casting include the bag, basket, or container used to store the bones and other objects. Bones and other objects used in casting must be stored safely in a container to protect both the physical and the spiritual elements. The bags can be made of soft materials to cushion any impacts. This is another aspect of the practice that needs to be personalized to suit your objects, practice, and worldview. Many different containers have been mentioned previously, including woven grass baskets and drawstring bags made from animal hide.

The type of bag or basket you choose will need to integrate into your practice seamlessly. Suppose you decide to use a shaking technique to mix and randomize the objects before casting them onto a surface. In that case, a basket may be the best option. However, if you prefer to select objects by drawing them randomly from a bag, an animal skin or fabric option would work best.

Many of the bags, baskets and other containers used to store bone-casting sets are elaborately decorated, with symbols importing magical properties. It is crucial to make this your own and impart your personal touches.

In some traditions, as among the Chokwe people, the bones are not cast onto a surface. Instead, as mentioned previously, the bones are shaken and randomized within the specially crafted divination basket. Wherever the objects come to land, within the basket, will be interpreted by the diviner.

FOUR

Collecting and Creating Your Own Bone Set

Finding Your Bones and Casting Items

CREATING YOUR OWN SET OF CASTING BONES IS A DEEPLY personal and ongoing project. Your practice and your bone set will constantly grow, change, and evolve as you develop new insights into your spiritual practice. As you heal and move on from old wounds and as you shift your focus towards new obstacles. This journey is not meant to have a set destination.

The first step in creating your own set of bones is sourcing all of the materials. There are a plethora of ready-made bone-casting sets available for purchase online. Many have been carefully researched and collated by experienced practitioners who take time and care in maintaining updated information and high-quality items. Ready-made bone sets are an excellent option for beginners that are still new to the practice. The sets often come with instructions and information booklets that you can refer to while casting.

You should examine these sets and remove any pieces you do not like or do not speak to you. You can also incorporate your own items into a pre-existing set. However, these options will not be suitable for everybody, especially not for experienced practitioners who benefit the most from creating their own collection.

There are many places you can start, one of the best places to look is in your own home. Many of us grew up collecting random assortments of items and curios. If you have managed to keep hold of these collections, take some time to rummage through them and see what you can find. You may have a box of gemstones collected during a childhood vacation or a package of sticks and stones from games you used to play. You can usually find a few precious items in such collections. Possessing an item and keeping it safe for years and years makes it unique and deeply personal; the item will contain an essence of your childhood spirit and curiosity.

Real Bones

There are four primary methods to use when finding real bones. The first is to source bones from the animal agriculture industry, either from a farmer, a slaughterhouse worker, a butcher, or a store. The second way is to hunt or kill an animal yourself, and the third way is to use your intuition to find bones from animals that have already died.

Buying Bones

The first method is perhaps the easiest way to get your hands on some animal bones. Unfortunately, there are a slew of ethical and moral issues with sourcing ritualistic or magical items in such a manner. By purchasing bones, you will have erased any possible connection with the spirit of the deceased animal. You will also be using the bones of an animal that has never lived a life of freedom, nor was their death honorable. The animals within the agriculture industry live under severe stress and abuse for the entire duration of their very short lives, receiving minimal veterinary care or compassion. Their bodies are scarred and tainted. If you use such bones in your practice, you will be inviting this negative energy into your life.

There is no way to ceremonially cleanse or bless the bones of an animal that has been commodified and exploited in such a way. They are not suitable for divination purposes.

If the only source of bones available to you is through the commercial sale of animal bodies, you can still attempt to use them. However, reparations must be made to the spirits of the deceased animals. You will need to communicate with the bones to figure out the best ways to do this, including saying a prayer for the animal spirit, making offerings and sacrifices, or carrying out specific rituals and ceremonies. A standard method of reparations is to bury the animal's remains in the ground, letting natural processes occur and allowing the animal spirit to settle. After a certain amount of time, depending on the animal spirit, you can exhume the remains and prepare them for a bone-casting set. This method is not guaranteed to work, as many animal spirits would not be willing to engage with the mortal world after their experiences.

Hunting

Another way to source bones for your casting set is to pursue, hunt, and kill a wild animal by yourself. Or get bones from another person that has killed the animal themselves. Depending on which part of the world you live in, you may have easy access to hunting grounds. You may be able to hunt without a permit during certain seasons. However, hunting permits are required in many countries and districts. You can apply for a hunting permit through your local organizations.

You can also opt to use the bones from a domestic animal such as a chicken. Your local laws will determine which options are available to you. There are some residential areas where you are legally allowed to slaughter livestock animals, but most regions bar this practice.

There are many cultural rituals and traditions associated with hunting. Since the dawn of civilization, people have made great efforts to ensure that animals are killed correctly.

This includes sourcing a free-range, wild animal that has not lived a life of imprisonment. This was the norm for much of human history; however, most animals on earth live inside factory farms in modern times. Humans have always hunted a wide range of animals, including large grazing herbivores such as deer and antelope, to smaller animals like birds, rabbits, and reptiles.

It is vital to select what kind of animal you would like to source bones from; this will affect all aspects of your practice. It must be personal, based on your own life experiences, desires, and intentions. For example, if you want to practice bone-casting to help your community deal with their various health issues, the bones of a lion or a bear would probably not be the most suitable. Large predators are not generally associated with healing abilities. Instead, the bones of a raven or a pig would be more practical, as these animals have been symbols of healing for many cultures. However, if you have a particularly lion-like personality where strength, courage, and determination are your defining characteristics, you would be better equipped to channel healing energy using lion bones.

Similarly, if you would like to practice bone-casting for fortune-telling purposes, you would want to avoid animals that represent bad luck, such as black cats. Still, suppose you have a deeply personal connection to any particular type of animal. In that case, that is important and relevant to your practice.

The process of tracking and hunting the animal is of vital importance. When taking a life, you must ensure it is done fairly. Using high-powered rifles with infra-red scopes from the safety of a vehicle is not a fair fight. Our ancestors could not afford to give their prey animals too many chances, but modern humans certainly can. It is best to use traditional hunting methods, relying on your skills and intuition to follow trails and track animal movements. Conventional weaponry such as a bow and arrow or blow darts would be most suitable.

People have used these methods to hunt and kill animals successfully for centuries.

In many religions, such as Islam, killing the animal with a blade to the throat is necessary. The cut must be made with a sharp knife that can sever the carotid arteries, jugular veins on both sides, and the windpipe, in one swift motion. When a Muslim person goes hunting, they cannot kill the animal with their weapons such as a gun or bow. Instead, they aim to wound and incapacitate the animal so that it can be safely approached, after which a blade is used to kill it along with ceremonial blessings and appeals to Allah. This is one of many nuances associated with taking the life of an animal. You must consult with your local practitioners and experts to determine how to go about taking an animal's life.

Agreements

You can obtain bones by receiving them as a gift or as a part of an agreed trade. Almost any bone is suitable if you accept them from another person. Much of the energy will have been altered, transmuted, and transformed by the previous user. You can even use human bones for bone casting if they have been gifted to you. However, you should take the time to check on your local laws regarding the use of human remains as it is illegal in many places. The bones of a direct ancestor would be most appropriate and respectful, especially if they could give their consent before death. Take time to connect with any human remains if you choose to use them. Ensure you try your best to learn their name and cultural heritage, learn about who their living descendants are, and find ways to pay respect and homage.

Leading with Intuition

The final option is perhaps the most common method people use to locate bones in the modern age. Bones can be found anywhere, from your back garden to the hiking trails in the mountains, to the roadside. If you spend enough time outside in the world looking for bones, you will eventually find them. Use your intuition to lead and guide you, travel and visit places you may not usually frequent, and listen to your gut. Manifest your intentions for finding bones in the world.

Bones can be sourced from any dead animals you find, including carcasses killed by another animal, roadkill, and individuals who have died from natural causes. You will need to take great care when dealing with bodies in various states of decay. Use gloves to handle the body, making sure nothing can pierce or scratch your skin. Use a respirator or a mask to avoid breathing in toxic gases produced by bacteria inside the body. Wash your hands thoroughly after handling any specimens to avoid contamination. Methods for preparing and treating the bones will be discussed later.

You can also use the bones from your pet! If a cherished pet passes away, their bodies are perfectly suitable for use in magical practices and divination. Your connection with their spirit will be strong, making them an excellent messenger between the living world and the spirit world. This can seem daunting to some, but it is a perfect way to maintain a living memory of your four-legged companions.

Human Bones

The use of human bones in ritual practices has always been controversial. Early human tribes have been found to use human skulls to create amulets. Pieces of the skull were carefully removed, and their edges cleaned up into smooth curves, with a hole to thread a string through. These amulets are believed to be created by the families of those who had died. They carried around the amulets to remember the deceased and to keep their memory alive. Various cultures have also used human bones in other elaborate types of jewelry, such as the Aztecs. They created necklaces and bracelets from the bones of their defeated enemies.

Buddhist, Tibetan, and Hindu people also have a history

of using human bones. They use skills to create ceremonial drinking cups, richly decorated and carved with intricate designs. These cups are used to make offerings such as water, wine, and food. The Buddhists also create flutes using the femur bones of humans. The music from these flutes is supposed to aid spirits in leaving the living world and severing their connection to materialism.

Bones have also been used to make weaponry. The human femur bone is extremely strong and can be used as a deadly weapon all on its own. Still, many cultures took to carving and shaping femur bones into sharp spears and blades. This stems from Paleolithic times, in which animal bones were used to create some of the first composite tools ever. Composite tools combined different materials such as bone, wood, and resins to make precise and accurate weaponry.

FIVE

Preparing a Bone-Casting Set

Now that you have successfully sourced the bones you would like to use in your bone-casting set, it is time to prepare them. This will involve physically cleaning the bones from the flesh and carrying out spiritual cleansing and blessing ceremonies. You will also be able to mark and personalize your bones and other items.

Decomposition

Decomposition is the natural process whereby organic materials are broken down into simpler compounds through bacteria, fungi, and animals. This process helps maintain the balance of life on Earth by constantly cycling and recycling nutrients and minerals. There are five stages of decomposition:

1. Fresh

This stage begins immediately after death. During this stage, the body will start to run out of oxygen, and the temperature will begin to drop. Rigor mortis will set in, causing the muscles and tissues to stiffen up. A build-up of carbon dioxide can break down cell membranes, releasing enzymes that begin breaking down the tissues. There will be no outward signs of decomposition yet, and the carcass should not have a foul smell, but flies may begin hovering and laying eggs.

2. Bloat

Anaerobic bacteria that live in the body and the gut begin to increase, producing potent gases such as ammonia, hydrogen sulfide, and methane which cause the body to swell and bloat. The body can double in size during this stage due to the pressure of the gas build-up. Foul gases are released in a process called putrefaction. The carcass should still be whole and intact at this stage if there were no wounds to the body.

3. Active Decay

The carcass will rupture during this stage due to the pressure from the bloating and deterioration of the flesh. Organisms such as beetles, flies, and worms will begin breaking down the larger pieces of flesh. At the same time, bacteria and fungi work on a soupy flurry of nutrients and minerals that leach into the ground. Soft tissues are broken down, while hard tissues remain.

4. Advanced Decay

Most of the decomposition activity has ceased by this point as nutrients from the carcass begin to run out. Fungal activity is high during this stage, with many spores being released. Bones and dry hide make up most of the remains. The remains are often discolored and blackened.

5. Skeletal Remains

The final stage of decomposition occurs when decomposers have removed all moisture and flesh. All that remains are the bones, with some hair, teeth, and claws. This is known as skeletonization.

Preparing Bones

There are many different methods that you can use to clean and prepare bones, depending on the state in which they are found. Below are methods for preparing bones from a fresh carcass; however, you can skip some of the steps if you have a dried carcass or dry bones. Note that this process can take days, weeks, or months depending on the size of your bones, the size of the animal, and the level of detail and intricacy that you are willing to work to. Following each of the steps outlined below will yield the best results; however, there are many variations that you can find online. Rushing the process of skipping steps will result in your bones having a bad rotting smell, and they may become stained yellow instead of bright white.

It is strongly recommended that you begin preparing and processing bones using a simple animal, such as a small mammal. Avoid rodents, birds, reptiles, and amphibians until you become more experienced. These types of animals have incredibly soft and delicate bones. Good starting animals include pet animals such as; cats or dogs, foxes, small pigs, raccoons, possums, mongoose or meerkats, monkeys, beavers, etc.

You will need the following tools:

- Your animal carcass or bones.
- Gloves that are waterproof and not easily torn.
- A plastic container large enough to fit the whole carcass.
- A pot or cooking container large enough to hold the carcass or bones.
- Hydrogen peroxide which is available as a liquid or as a cream/paste.
- Liquid hydrogen peroxide usually comes in 2% concentrations.

- Peroxide cream usually comes in stronger concentrations, about 40%.
- Chlorine bleach which used in household cleaning:
- Biological laundry detergent can be used in place of bleach.
- Water.
- Rags, old scraps of fabric for wiping messes.
- Scrubbing brush depending on the size of your carcass, but toothbrushes or nail brushes will work.
- Tweezers.
- Tongs to handle hot bones and flesh.
- Time and patience.

The first step is to carry out some basic processing of the carcass. If you have the know-how, you can skin the corpse. However, your main goal is to gently remove as much flesh as possible without damaging the skeleton. You can disembowel the animal and throw out the innards if need be. Avoid using knives at this stage, as you may sever important ligaments that hold the bones together.

The next step is to allow decomposition to take place using a dry burial.

For a dry burial, it is helpful to place the carcass into a stocking or pantyhose. This will help ensure you can manage all tiny pieces that break away, such as teeth, claws, finger bones, and vertebrae. Make some small holes in the stockings to allow insects to travel in and out. Use an old rag to wrap around the stocking. You will need to dig a hole in the ground, large enough to fit the entire carcass without touching. Cover the floor and brace the sides of the hole with boards or rags to prevent collapsing. Then place the wrapped carcass into the hole. Cover the top to protect it from the elements and scavengers; chicken mesh or something similar is appropriate. You can also palace a large rock on top to further dissuade scavengers. Then simply allow time to pass. You will rely on the natural processes of decomposition, which include bacteria and fungi growth and the influx of insects such as carrion beetles, flies, and their maggots. You can purchase carrion beetles directly from some pet stores to speed up the process.

Check on the carcass regularly. You will leave the corpse in this hole until it reaches the skeletal stage. There should be no putrid smells coming from the carcass, though there should be mold. You can also use above-ground containers for this stage, but ensure they are placed far from your home to avoid odors and pathogens.

You can also use a dry burial method to get it completely dry if you already have a semi-dry carcass.

The next step is to remove the flesh from the bones. Exhume the carcass and remove it from the wrappings. You will need to be extremely delicate from this stage onwards. Gently tease apart the limbs and structures so that you can remove the bones. Place them into a large container filled with cold, soapy water and bleach. You can use the natural laundry detergent for this stage as soap. If the flesh is too rigid and the bones are stuck, allow the carcass to soak in the soapy water for a few hours or days, depending on your needs. You should then be able to use your hands to work at the bones.

The skull and spinal cord can be tough to work with; do not worry if there are still pieces of flesh on these bones, you can still move onto the next step once you have removed everything you can.

Once you have successfully removed all of the bones from the flesh, you can begin disinfecting them. However, if there are still pieces of flesh stuck to the bones, you may need to simmer them in water for a few hours. Strictly avoid boiling the bones, as the movement within the pot from the bubbles can lead to damage. However, even simmering is not the best method and is used only when the process needs to be rushed because heating the bones can become warped and distorted.

Next, rinse the bones in clean water to remove any bleach.

If you leave the bones in bleach for too long, they will begin to turn yellow. Then, set them out to dry. At this point, most if not all of the flesh should be gone. However, you can use a toothbrush to remove any final pieces.

Use a scrubbing brush to scrub each of the bones with cold soapy water. Make sure you scrub the entire surface to remove microscopic bacteria as well, not just the nooks and crannies. You may notice that the bones are still covered in an oily substance. A biological detergent should strip all of these oils, but if not, soak them in cold soapy water overnight.

The hydrogen peroxide step comes next. Create a solution of hydrogen peroxide and water. Make it as strong as possible to speed up the process. A 1:1 ratio of water to peroxide is good. Make sure you have enough solution to submerge your bones in a plastic container completely. You should immediately notice tiny bubbles forming on the surface of the bone once it is submerged. You can leave the bones to soak in this solution for up to 24 hours.

The final step is to allow the bones to dry completely. Set them out to dry in a cool, dark place like a pantry. Avoid getting the bones hot as they will crack or become warped. You will now have a complete skeleton for use in your bone-casting practices. You can try to rearticulate the skeleton for display purposes.

Alternatives

If you do not have the time or the space to bury the bodies of the dead animals, you can choose to boil them instead. This method will work faster but can lead to lower quality results at the end of the process. Instead of burying the carcass and allowing decomposition to occur naturally, you can gently boil it in a large pot. Boil the carcass whole, with all the body parts intact. The flesh will begin to soften and readily fall away from the bones. This can take up to a few days, depending on the size. Avoid rapidly boiling water and use a low simmer instead.

Cleansing and Blessing Bones

With a collection of freshly cleaned and prepared bones, you are ready to start the next step of your bone-casting journey. Whenever you work with spiritual energies and magical practices such as divination, you must take the time to cleanse and bless your tools properly.

Cleansing your bones does not involve scrubbing them with soap and water like you would when preparing them. Cleansing is a spiritual and magical practice in which negative energies are cleansed and removed from your tools. Cleansing must be carried out to ensure that your bones are not possessed by negative energies or entities that may wish you harm. Negative energy can result in blockages or stagnation in the channeling abilities to cast bones, and other such magical tools, making them ineffective at divination.

There are many different ways to cleanse bones and tools using many other methods. A key factor in all cleansing rituals is your intentions. You must make your intentions known by meditating on them, speaking them out loud, or writing them down. For a cleansing ritual, your intentions should revolve around the removal and banishment of any negativity.

Water

One of the simplest methods of cleansing is using water. Keeping your intentions in mind at all times, gently rinse your bones and tools in clean and cool water. You can use any type of clean water, whether it comes from a tap or from a mountain spring, and whether it has been blessed or not. You may have some bones that are particularly dry and porous, as well as other objects that shouldn't get wet if you can help it. For these types of objects, you can use other methods of cleansing.

Salt

Another method is to use salt for cleansing purposes. Salt has a fantastic ability to absorb energy, be it positive, neutral or negative. You can use absolutely any kind of salt in your cleansing rituals. Himalayan salt is often marketed and touted as a premium product. Still, it is no different than table salt or rock salt. You can use salt by sprinkling it over your bones and tools, but a better method is to construct a simple salt bath in which you can submerge your tools. You can also use rock lamps and place your objects close by. You do not need to make a salt solution as dry salt is recommended. Again, keep your intentions in mind as you allow your tools to soak in the salt bath for as long as you think is necessary. The salt will not cause any chemical damage to your bones.

It is common practice to incorporate plants, herbs, and resins into a salt or water bath. You can select cleansing herbs or resins such as blue sage, cedar, cinnamon, rosemary, juniper, frankincense, myrrh, sandalwood, cypress, lavender, thyme, or pine. Herbs can be used fresh or dried, powders or infused into oils, or even in incense.

Earth

Magical tools can be cleaned using dirt from the Earth. This may seem counterintuitive, and you may not wish to see your prized collection of bones returning to the ground. However, the Earth has a remarkable ability to cleanse spiritual energy. Simply bury your tools in a shallow hole or cover them in a container filled with dirt. Allow them to remain buried for a few days.

Air

Similar to using salt or dirt, you can cleanse your tools using fresh air. Keep your intentions in mind as you use wind or your own breath to quickly and easily blow away any unwanted energy. Breath is a widespread tool used by all kinds of spiritual practitioners.

Sun and Moon

The sun and the moon are the most important celestial bodies in the sky. The sun is the most potent force in the entire solar system. The moon acts as a mirror, reflecting its energy into the nighttime. You can quickly cleanse your objects by soaking them in the sunshine or the moonlight. They will work to eradicate any negative energies or entities and drive them away. If you are going to leave your objects out during the day or overnight, make sure they are protected from scavenging animals. Keep in mind that many objects can become damaged by prolonged exposure to sunlight, including bones. Avoid leaving them out for more than a few hours at a time.

Smoke

Smoke is also used in cleansing ceremonies. You can burn dried leaves, herbs, or grass and waft the smoke over your magical tools and bones while keeping your intentions in the forefront of your mind. The smoke will help to elevate and lift away any negative energies, carrying them away. Though many herbs are used for traditional cleansing purposes, you are free to use any herbs that call to you. You will know they call you if you enjoy them!

To burn herbs, you will need to dry them and then create tight little bundles. Ignite one end of the bundle and blow out the flames so that only an ember remains. You can wave the bundle around to distribute the smoke evenly, and you can blow the smoke into different directions to clear out corners or difficult-to-reach places. You do not need to burn the entire bundle; only a few wafts of smoke will suffice for most cases. Ensure to properly extinguish the bundle when you are finished and store it in a cool, dark place.

Some of the most commonly used plants in magical circles include blue sage, mugwort, sandalwood, frankincense, vervain, mint, lavender, rosemary, basil, bay, cinnamon, cardamon, clove, jasmine, juniper, patchouli, St John's wort, wormwood, nutmeg, and rose.

Smudging

Smudging is a specific type of smoke cleansing ritual used by the native people of South, Central, and North America. The primary plants used include palo santo and white sage.

Palo santo is produced from the bark of trees with the same name, but resins and oils are also extracted. White sage is a type of sage that is indigenous to the Americas. These herbs are of the utmost importance to the American people, and they are strictly protected. Many practitioners advise against using such herbs unless you are a part of Native American culture. Due to the appropriation of many indigenous practices, these plants are at risk of extinction due to unsustainable and ecologically damaging harvesting practices.

A comparable tradition is practiced by Zulu sangomas using a herb called mphepho (imphepho). This plant is considered one of the most important and most powerful spiritual agents. However, it is not generally used for cleansing purposes. Instead, it is a device of communication with the spirit world. It is supposed to be used exclusively by trained sangomas. Suppose untrained persons use the herb without the correct ceremonies, rituals, and procedures. In that case, they risk opening themselves up to possession from harmful spiritual entities. This is mainly because untrained practitioners have not strengthened their connection with their ancestors, who offer protection in the spirit world.

Essential Oils

Essential oils are concentrated plant extracts, and they can be used to cleanse magical objects such as tools and bones. You can select any type of herb or plant that you enjoy or use the traditional cleansing varieties. Take care when applying oils to real bone, though. Bones will absorb the moisture and the oils, which can lead to the formation of stains. Essential oils can also be burned or used to anoint objects.

Crystals

Crystals are unique manifestations of the Earth's vibrational energy. They are formed through the immense temperatures and pressures under the surface, where elements are crushed and packed into neatly organized shapes and structures. Many crystals have profound cleansing abilities due to their internal structures, which can transmute negative energy. However, not all crystals are effective in cleansing. Clear quartz is always a primary candidate, with the transparency highlighting the cleaning abilities. Amethysts are richly colored purple crystals that can be used in cleansing. They serve to absorb negative energy from objects as opposed to absorbing or altering it.

High-Frequency Sounds

You may have heard the mantra 'om' before being prevalent in the Hindu and Buddhist religions. The rhythmic chanting of the word is used as a spiritual tool, replicating the primordial sound of the vibrating universe. High-frequency sounds can be used to elevate the vibrational energy that exists in all objects. You can use these frequencies to cleanse your magical tools. You can use your voice through chants such as 'om.' You can clap your hands with intention. You can also use instruments; playing your favorite song or striking a bell will shift and transmute the negative energy. You can also use singing bowls, which are traditional to the Tibetan people who practice Buddhism.

Banishing vs. Cleansing vs. Purification

These terms are often used interchangeably in esoteric circles; however, there are distinct and essential differences. As mentioned, cleansing is a normal process in which unwanted energies are removed from magical tools and objects. Cleansing is a personal process relating to the energies you sense and that you want to be removed. Purification is a similar practice. The aim is not to cleanse items for personal use but to carry out purification in a predefined and ritualistic manner, following the steps outlined in cultural traditions. Purification is carried out less often than cleansing, which should be done regularly. If you are not a part of a long line of cultural practitioners, you may not have any need for purification rituals.

Banishing is also a similar practice to cleansing. It aims to remove more powerful and potentially malevolent spirits, such as demons or fae, from inhabiting and possessing your tools, your space, or your person. Banishing often involves more ritualistic practices than essential cleansing ceremonies, usually with a team of practitioners who actively work to rid spirits and demons.

Blessing the Bones

Now that you have successfully cleaned your bones and your magical tools of unwanted energy, you can begin to impart your own energy back into the objects. You bless your objects following any methods that suit you, your practice, and your cultural heritage. Blessings serve not only to impart positive energy but also to protect the user.

In the Wiccan tradition, it is customary to cast a circle to carry out magical activities. The circle is used to protect the practitioner from negative entities and amplify the magical work they are carrying out. The first step to cast a circle is to identify a suitable space in which you can work. It needs to be big enough to sit comfortably, along with all of your tools and bones, and free from interference from other people. Next, identify and mark out the cardinal directions; north, south, east, and west. Candles are used as traditional markers. It is also customary to pair each cardinal direction with one of the classical elements. A standard configuration pairing sees north and Earth, east and air, south and fire, west and water. You can place a representative object next to each candle. For example, after laying out the four candles, place a small bowl of water next to the west candle. Place a small bowl of dirt next to the north candle. Place a small empty bowl (representing air) next to the east candle. Last, place a stick of incense next to the south candle. You can physically draw the circle onto the ground, use crayons or other kinds of stationery, or you can sprinkle dirt, flowers, seeds, etc. Any type of object that can be sprinkled to form a line is suitable. It is traditional to draw in a clockwise direction, starting by facing north.

Salt is very commonly used for this purpose, but this is strongly advised against it unless you plan to clean it all up. Salt leaches into soils and poisons them, making it impossible for plants to grow. The term 'salting the Earth' highlights the seriousness of salt toxicity.

Now you can begin 'casting' your circle. Start by starting at the north candle, lighting it, speaking an incantation, and moving in a clockwise direction to light the east, south, and west candle. Each time you should speak an incantation to manifest your intentions for blessing your objects. You can use any type of incantation; you simply need to speak your intentions out loud. Once you have lit each candle, you can begin meditating on the objects. Sit inside the circle and hold each of your magical tools while keeping your intentions in mind. Infuse them with your spiritual energy by envisioning it as smoke or essence that travels from your body into the objects. Once you are done, you can begin closing the circle. To do this, blow out the candles in the same clockwise direction as before.

Casting a circle is only one way to bless bones, and it is not a requirement. You can bless your bones safely by holding them or hovering your hand above them and praying, or manifest your intentions by speaking them out loud. You can sleep with your bones, bathe with them, work, or play with them. Any ritualistic process that is deeply connected to you as a person will work.

Marking the Bones

Bones can be marked in a plethora of different ways, including naming them. You can use markings to personalize your tools and bones. Still, you can also use markings to make identification more straightforward and to speed up the process of reading and interpreting the bones. You can use any type of tools to make markings, including basic pens, pencils, and crayons, paints and dyes, jewels and decorations, carvings, and inscriptions using a gouge.

Naming your objects will help you become more familiar with their shape and feel, making your readings faster and more efficient. You will not need to try and figure out which bone is which and what meaning is assigned to which piece. You do not need to write the names down onto the bones themselves; the act of giving a name is sufficient.

You can also use physical markings. Colors are an excellent tool and work well on bones. You can paint the tips or the entire bone. You can use the different colors to represent different meanings. For example, a wishbone in a set could represent luck, wealth, and fortune. It would make sense to color such a bone in green, commonly associated with these characteristics. Similarly, you can use the color red for the more potent pieces in your set or shades of grey and different tones.

You can also use symbols, dots, or other types of markings. Markings can be drawn on, painted on, or carved into the surface of the bones. There are so many potential symbols you could use. It is best to use markings that resonate with your personality. If you are particularly interested in working with Norse mythology, you could mark your bones with runes.

Bones and other casting items can also be decorated in different ways, such as using beadwork, jewels, gems and stones, teeth and claws, or fur, as well as holes or cracks. You can use glue to stick decorations onto your bones, but ensure you use acid-free glue to avoid yellow stains from forming.

SIX

Caring and Feeding Your Bones

NOW THAT YOU HAVE A BEAUTIFULLY PREPARED, CLEANED, AND blessed set of casting bones, you can begin to use them in your practice. You will need to take care of them, as bones are delicate objects, especially smaller ones, and they may become damaged over time. If a bone should break, there are a few ways to interpret this occurrence. In many circles of practitioners, a piece that breaks has served its purpose and should be discarded. You can throw bones into the trash, you can store them in an air-tight container, or you return them to the Earth by burying them. However, in different circles, broken pieces can represent the embracing of flaws and imperfections. The Japanese practice of kintsugi is an excellent way to highlight such a worldview. Kintsugi is a method of repairing objects, primarily pottery, using molten gold to join the pieces back together. The end product is arguably more beautiful, stunning, and has more character than the original, thanks to conserving and repairing it. Casting bones can be repaired using kintsugi or similar methods.

The bones will need to be inspected for damage regularly. Check the surfaces for any minute cracks, fractures, or chips. You can use a clear nail-polish enamel to make minimal cosmetic touch-ups, but the chemicals can cause the bones to stain yellow over time.

Bones should not be exposed to high levels of humidity, sunlight, or temperature changes. It is best to store them in a cool, dark place such as a cupboard. You can keep them in plastic, cardboard, wooden, or metal containers, but wrap them in fabric first.

Feeding

You will also need to feed your bones. You may be wondering why the dead remains of an animal would need to be fed. Still, if you wish for the animal's spirit to linger and play a role in your practice, you will need to keep them happy. Feeding involves making offerings to the animal spirits associated with each of your bones, as well as other animal objects such as shells, claws, teeth, fur, or hide.

It is up to you to determine what to feed your bones and how often to feed them. This will be based on the type of animal that the bones come from and how often you use them in your practice. To make an offering, you should lay out your bones somewhere that has been cleared and cleaned for this purpose. Altars will work. Set the offering next to the bone. Either speak your intentions aloud or meditate on them in your mind. Connect the spirit of the animal with your offering.

Offerings can include food items. You can offer a piece of dried meat if you practice with the bones of a carnivore, or you could offer fresh grass if you use bones from a grazer. Food items will need to be removed and discarded eventually. The spirit will not eat the food itself; instead, it will feed on the energy, so food products will rot and decompose. However, it is not very common to encounter animal spirits that request food items.

You can also make offerings in the form of other objects,

such as gems, stones, jewels, rocks, salt, herbs, plants, insects, etc. Absolutely anything is suitable, but whether or not the animal spirits will accept them is to be determined by yourself. You can use trial and error during this process, but always offer the utmost respect to the spirit and apologize if they reject the offering. Some examples include offering the bones of a raven many different shiny objects. Something they would have been happy to collect when they were alive. Offering the bones of a cat, a sun catcher to represent warm sunshine. Offering insects to the spirit of a bat or offering the bones of a mouse a small, safe box in which it could find safety. You get the idea.

Some animal spirits will accept non-material offerings such as promises or placements. For example, a lion spirit may accept an offer of great sacrifice on your part, such as giving up a certain kind of food or setting aside time to practice your craft every single day. The spirit of a beloved pet may accept kindness and compassion towards other animals as a form of offering.

If you are unsure about what kind of offerings to make to your animal spirits, you can always ask them by casting the bones. They will communicate with you through the bones, and you can work with them to find an answer. It is helpful to offer them a few options and let them decide. You will know that your offering has been rejected if it breaks or becomes tarnished in odd ways. Rejected offerings tend to be devoid of energy, and you can use your intuition to determine whether they should be thrown out or not.

How often to feed your bones will be determined by how often you practice and the type of animal spirit. High energy animals such as birds may require feeding weekly, compared to a reptilian spirit that may only need to feed once a year. Most mammal spirits would be appeased with a monthly or seasonal offering. However, if you practice often, you will need to feed them more often.

Storing Your Bones

Divination bones must be stored carefully and correctly to prevent them from becoming physically or spiritually damaged. Bones can be extremely fragile, especially smaller bones. They will tend to become more fragile over time as they become drier as well. To protect your bones from physical damage, you should store them in soft fabric or hide wrappings with a string to secure the bundle. Be sure that the bones cannot fall out of the bundle, but do not overtighten the string as you may break the bones. You can store the bundle within another piece of wrapping or within a plastic sheet. Place your bundles within a safe box or a hard container such as a closet. They must always be stored within a cool, dark place. This will keep your bones safe from damage from impacts, exposure to the elements, and insects.

If you have a divination bag or basket specially crafted for use in bone-casting ceremonies, you can use these containers to store your bones. However, the bags and baskets will deteriorate and become damaged over time, but you can make efforts to reduce this. Treat the objects with care. Make efforts not to bend or misshape the objects and avoid messing with liquids, oils, or food products.

To keep the spiritual energy within your bones safe when not in use, you can use markings, sigils, or other types of symbols on your wrapping materials or container. There are thousands of different symbols from hundreds of different world cultures that you can use. The Christian cross is an example of a protective symbol used daily by millions of people across the globe.

You can also keep your bones safe without the need for any protective symbols or sigils by seeing that your home and your practice space are cleaned regularly. This will help to ensure no negative entities enter into or dwell within your area. Therefore they cannot affect the bones.

SEVEN

Entering Into a Relationship with Your Bones

To successfully use any magical object, you must create a connection with its spirit and energy first. This is exceptionally important for those who do not come from cultures that venerate ancestors. There is no preexisting link or connection for the spirit to work with or identify. Those who practice ancestor worship may not have to work so hard to create relationships with their bones and tools as long as they maintain a strong connection with their ancestors.

Meditation

Bone casters and diviners of all kinds need to enter into a relationship with their bones before they can begin casting. This involves opening up a spiritual dialogue with the bones in which you discuss the terms and conditions of your practice. Also, the role of the bones within your practice. Some important aspects that need to be determined include which animal spirits are associated with your bones. What kind of expectations you may have of the spirits, and what expectations they may have for you. This includes the type of outcomes you would expect during a casting ceremony or what kind of offerings the bones may expect in return.

Meditation is the most effective method to use when trying to enter into a relationship with your bones and their spirits. Meditation does not need to involve any specific processes or religious rituals. It does not require chanting or hallucinogenic drugs. It does not require a guide. To meditate, all that is needed is a quiet place where you can relax in peace; you can stand, sit or lie down, with your eyes closed or open. It is entirely up to you to decide how you want to meditate. Use your intuition to uncover methods that you enjoy and that are effective for you. Discard practices that have not shown benefits, and focus on those that bring you positivity.

There are many broad categories of meditation, including mindfulness, spiritual, focused, movement, and mantra meditation. The aim of mindfulness practices is to become more present, to exist in the here and now without wasting time and energy wondering about the past or the future. Mindfulness involves silencing the typical dialogue in your mind, including all of the worries and stresses of daily life. During a meditation session, you will sit or lie in a quiet place and allow your thoughts to flow over you like water in a stream. Do not linger on any thoughts, do not get sidetracked into imagining different scenarios or what could have been. Let the thoughts appear, and move on. As you sit, try to take note of the general theme in your thoughts. For example, if you notice that again and again, you come back to thoughts of housework, overdue bills, or looming deadlines, take note of the fact that you are probably under more stress than you realize.

Likewise, if you notice that your thoughts keep bringing you back to a specific memory or worry, do take note, but do not linger. Keep bringing your attention back to the present moment, where you are, how you feel, what you hear, what you smell, etc. Keep yourself grounded in the here and now. After much practice, you may begin to notice that it is easier to silence your thoughts, and it becomes easier to stay in the present moment.

Focused meditations are carried out for specific purposes, such as connecting with your bones. To carry out a focused meditation, you will still need to sit or lie in a quiet and peaceful place, one in which you feel safe and secure, and your bones can be spread out close at hand. You can light candles or burn incense; you can play music or listen to the silence. You are welcome to carry out cleansing rituals before you begin a meditation, though this is not a requirement. Take your bones into your hands, or hover your hands above the bones, and meditate on them for a few minutes at a time. Picture the bone in your mind's eye, imagine the weight and feel, shape and colors, smell, and other characteristics. Be quiet, and allow the bones to speak for themselves. You can use your intuition to determine which thoughts may be stemming from a source other than yourself. The bones will attempt to communicate to you their needs, desires, and wants.

Focused Meditation Questions

Some important questions to consider during your meditations include:

1. What kind of animal spirit are the bones possessed by?

2. What kind of questions can I ask of this bone?

3. How will the spirit communicate?

A. Will the spirit communicate using bones alone, or other methods as well, such as sending signs and messages or communicating through dreams?

4. Can the bones offer insight into the past or the future, or are they concerned with the present moment?

5. Which dimension of wellness is the bone concerned with?

A. Will this bone be concerned with my body and physical health?

B. Will this bone help to stimulate and challenge my mind?

C. Will this bone serve to understand, regulate and manage my emotions?
D. Will this bone be concerned with my society and community issues?
E. Will this bone be concerned with my spirit?
F. Will this bone help in finding my purpose in life?
G. Will this bone guide me through financial problems?
H. Will this bone serve the environment?

6. What kind of rituals should be performed for the bones, and how often?
7. What kind of offerings are expected of the bones?
8. How often should I make offerings?
9. How can I know that the bone is communicating with me?
10. What kind of patterns, formations, and configurations will the bones form when answering my questions?
11. How should I interpret different patterns, formations, and configurations?
12. What kind of energy can you expect to feel when working with the bone?
A. Will the spirit channel good, neutral, or evil energy?
B. Is this a trickster spirit?

This is not an exhaustive list but should give you a good idea of the type of questions you should try and focus on during your meditations. You will need to go through this process for each bone in your set. You can also do this with non-bone items. However, they are doubtful to be possessed by a specific animal spirit whose qualities and characteristics can be usefully channeled.

After carrying out many focused meditation sessions, you should have a much stronger relationship with your bones. You should have a good understanding of the spiritual energy possessed by each of the items. You should be able to identify the animal spirits and the type of energy you can work with, the type of problems that are willing to engage and help you with, and the type of reparations expected in return.

Talk to the Bones

One of the easiest methods to connect with your bones without sitting still in a quiet place for extended periods is simply talking to them. You can speak to the bones about how your day went. About your wants and desires. About your fears and apprehensions, or any other topic. This allows the spirits inhabiting the bones to get to know you better. They can figure out your place within society and determine what kind of person you are. The bones will not be very entertaining conversationalists, but they are excellent listeners.

Working with Them Regularly

You can build a relationship with your bones by working with them regularly. Use them for casting, even if just to practice or to get a better idea of which techniques feel right to you. You can use your bones to test out many different mixing and casting methods and different reading and interpretation methods. Through continued use, the bones will be able to learn more about you as a practitioner. They will be able to give you confirmation for your current methods, or they can suggest alternatives that may be better suited. The bones will be able to pick up on the purposes of your divination practice, and they will be able to serve as more efficient lines of communication with the spirit world. Just as you gain experience through practice, so too will the bones.

Carrying Them on Your Person

You can also carry your bones, or one particular bone, around with you as you carry out your day-to-day tasks such as going to work or cleaning the house. Skin-to-bone contact can be very powerful and can rapidly strengthen a connection with the bones and the practitioner. The bones will be able to detect and feel your own spiritual energy, allowing them to mold and fit themselves into your practice. You can carry your bones in your pocket or a bag; you can also carry them inside a bra or within a special pouch. It is common to create temporary jewelry pieces, carry your bones, and keep them safe. Still, they can be easily removed and used in a casting ritual. You can carry bones on your person for as long as it feels right to you, whether just through the course of the day or for longer stretches.

Note that this method will transfer your energy. If you have a bad day, that negativity can become an integral part of a bone. This is not a problem, and you can carry out cleansing rituals at the end of a bad day. Similarly, take a bone with you on an extraordinary journey or during an important experience. The bone will take up your energy. For example, suppose you climbed Mount Kilimanjaro while carrying a precious piece of bone. In that case, that bone will forever be infused with your hard work, determination. As well as the essence of the mountain and its challenges.

Keep in mind that bodily fluids may cause damage to your bones. Sweat, blood, and urine may cause discoloration, and excess moisture can cause bones to crack.

Sleeping with the Bones

This method is a highly effective means of creating a strong relationship with your bones. When in a dream state, your subconscious mind can run freely, expressing all of your thoughts, desires, fears, and intentions without inhibition. Dreams serve as a fantastic means of gaining insight into a person's mind. The bones will be able to detect changes in your energy as you dream and sleep. They can pick up on scenarios you wish to avoid or experiences you want to have. Sleeping with your bones is also an excellent way to 'recharge' them and reinvigorate their energy alongside your own. Place the bones on a bedside table. You can also put them under your pillow, within a pillowcase or duvet cover, or under your mattress. If you simply place the bones under a blanket, there is a high chance of them breaking or falling off the bed.

Blood Offerings

One of the most ancient forms of offerings includes precious items such as food and water and essential life-giving blood. Blood is one of the most personal and meaningful offerings that a person can make; it represents life, fertility, and sacrifice. Blood must be given freely, without coercion. This can be seen in many cultures worldwide that have participated in human sacrifice; people must volunteer for the sacrifice to be venerated. Nobody can be forced to offer blood or their life, as the spirits will not accept this. There are some exceptions in which the gods of religion are particularly bloodthirsty; this is most common in war faring cultures, such as the ancient Aztecs. The Aztecs made massive human sacrifices to the god Huitzilopochtli. They believed this would help prevent the end of the world. They sacrificed volunteers, but also prisoners captured during warfare. The Aztecs engaged in wars for the express purpose of collecting more people for sacrifices.

Blood offerings should not be taken lightly, as they are potent and binding. First, make sure you use sterile instruments if you are going to make incisions in your own flesh. Second, properly dispose of any instruments that have come into contact with blood, such as tissues, gloves, and sharps, including blades, needles, or lances. You only need a few drops of blood at most. Once you have the blood, you can use it as an offering as is, or you can infuse the blood into candles, tonics, essential oils, etc. You can also write out spells or symbols using blood. You can also use the blood to anoint and bless objects. Menstrual blood is suitable for any practice that requires blood, and many believe it holds even more feminine energy and power than normal blood. Blood offerings and any blood magic practices are powerful and should only be used for serious issues. Irresponsible use of blood can lead to your power and energy being stolen or transmuted by external forces, such as demons or benign spirits. Do not consume blood in any form, as this can lead to medical issues and spiritual issues.

Maintenance

A part of building a relationship with your bones is maintaining them by inspecting them and looking for cracks, chips, and fractures, or other damage, and making efforts to mend or release the bones from your care. This has been mentioned previously, but the longer you can keep a bone within your set, the more powerful and prominent it will become. A major aspect of spiritual maintenance is carrying out cleansing and blessing ceremonies regularly to clear out stagnant energy and replenish it with new invigorating energy. This also involves the methods you use to store and feed your bones. Ensure they are safe both physically and spiritually.

EIGHT

What Questions Are Best For Bone Readings?

The Nature of Questions

BONES ARE OPEN TO ANSWERING ALMOST ANY TYPE OF question you can think of, unlike other forms of divination, which are often suited to a specific kind of question. This is due to the nature of bone casting; a set of bones contains many different types of bones with different meanings associated with each piece. Numerous bones will be thrown during a casting, leading to a more nuanced, complete reading. In contrast, other divination practices, such as tarot, also have many cards with different meanings. But they are not cast simultaneously. Usually, no more than nine tarot cards are used during a reading. Bones can be used to answer broad and open-ended questions or precise questions. Bones are also particularly good at answering sequential questions that lead on from one another instead of using a series of unrelated questions.

However, the nature of the question is an essential aspect of any divination practice. The nature of the question can reveal the mental state and mindset of the practitioner or their client. For example, a question such as 'when will my suffering end?' shows a great deal of turmoil in the person's life. They likely need the support of other forms, such as medical support or support from friends and family, before they begin turning to divination. The idea of a 'Law of Attraction' also comes into play—a person focused only on the negative aspects of their life will attract further negativity. Instead, questions used for bone-casting and any form of divination should concentrate on the desired outcome rather than the problem. For example, ask 'what can I do to improve my health?' instead of 'when will my suffering end?'.

Also important to keep in mind is that bone casting is a practice that heavily relies on animal spirits for guidance. Animal spirits are sincere and blunt; they do not need a metaphor or long-winded symbolism. Instead, they will be as direct as possible, cutting to the chase. For example, if you ask the bones why you can't achieve success. In that case, they will likely blame you as a person rather than circumstances or challenges. This is important to remember when reading your castings.

Suitable Questions

Bone-casting is not a form of fortune-telling, and it cannot be used to predict the future. The bones can only offer insight gathered by forces in the spirit world. Therefore, any questions of such a nature would not be suitable and would not provide any meaningful answers. This includes questions relating to prophecy, gambling, or death, such as 'when will I die?'

Bone-casting is a suitable divination practice for 'yes' or 'no' questions. However, the bones may provide you with only a 'yes' or 'no' answer, offering no insight or additional information. By assigning a bone to represent 'yes' or 'no' answers and casting it along with the rest of the pieces in the set, you may be able to gain more context and information from the spirits regarding your 'yes' or 'no' question.

Bone-casting is also suitable for questions about time, unlike other methods. Bones can be incorporated into a set to represent the past or the future, or your throwing surface could be marked with different sections representing the past, present, and future. The bones are good at making sense of events, including their causation and the effects of the events. Depending on how you choose to assign meaning to your bones, you can receive precise answers about different times and circumstances.

The best type of questions to ask the bones would be open-ended questions that can be answered using several different pieces in your set. Combining different bones and objects helps create a fuller and more representative answer that you can read and interpret. Questions such as 'What can I do to become happier?', 'When will my career begin to take off?' or 'How can I deal with my anxiety in a better way?' make excellent questions in which the spirits of the bones can really try to find you a nuanced answer with many different potential solutions.

Questions to Avoid

There are some types of questions that you want to avoid. The bones can definitely be used to aid and improve healing. But they cannot offer you medical advice or diagnoses. This is not in their skill set or knowledge base. Other types of highly specific questions will also not work. You cannot ask the bones to identify the location of hidden treasure. Expose the name of someone interested in you, or tell you the exact date and time of a child's birth.

People will often ask questions that they do not actually want the answers to. This is because the responses may be hurtful. The person is not psychologically prepared to deal with the issue yet. These types of questions should not be asked during bone-casting. The bones may provide the answer you have avoided, leading to emotional turmoil, pain, and suffering. Sometimes it is best not to know and prepare yourself for the outcomes in the meantime. An example could include the spouse of a cheating partner; they may want to know why their spouse is cheating. The cheating partner may no longer be in love with their spouse, and this can cause far more pain than the act of infidelity.

Bone-casting should not be used to answer questions that you already know the answers to. It is common for people to avoid answers when it means they have to take accountability or action. Therapies such as cognitive-behavioral therapies have proven to be very effective in helping people deal with psychological barriers. However, bone-casting is not an alternative to therapy, where the client sits back. At the same time, the therapist lists all the problems and solutions. Instead, bone casting is a form of guidance that can help you develop your own therapeutic strategies for dealing with the issues in your life.

Similarly, bone casting should answer questions that you actually care about and which affect your life. Do not ask the bones trivial questions or common knowledge. The bones may entertain a few unimportant questions if you have developed a good relationship with them. All the same, the spirits will quickly tire and become bored. Equally as important, do not pose questions to test the spirits. They will not appreciate this. They may become angered and spiteful or choose to disconnect from you permanently. Rendering your bones useless and your own spirit unprotected. Testing the spiritual abilities of your bones is a blatant sign of disrespect to the spirits.

The bones cannot be used to pry into the lives of others; they will not provide gossip or interesting tidbits about your fellow community members. You cannot use bone-casting to find out the personal information of another person. The only types of questions that you can ask about others must revolve around your relationship with that person. For example, you cannot ask the bones to tell you about your mother's health condition. However, you can ask the bone to help you improve your relationship with your mother so that she may willingly and voluntarily share her health concerns with you unprompted.

Finally, avoid repetitive questions. If you have come to the bones hoping that they would answer your specific question, but they do not give you an answer, you should definitely try one or two more times. However, any more would be a waste of time. The bones have decided that they are unable or unwilling to answer this question. Do not try to rephrase it or ask multiple times over; the outcome will not change. The spirits will only engage with topics that interest them and are considered important. Often, the issues facing mortals on the surface of the Earth are not regarded as pressing or important to the spirit world. This does not mean you should also avoid sequential questions that lead on from each other. The spirit can be mainly instrumental when dealing with questions that provide more context to a situation.

The Best Type of Question

The best type of question to ask during a bone-casting ceremony is an open-ended question. Even more so if you have spent some time meditating on your question. You should already have a good idea of the potential outcomes that may arise. You should take the time to consider and weigh each likely outcome before casting bones. This helps the spirits develop a better understanding of your question and its context within your life at the present moment. Being open-ended also means that the bones can offer you a more detailed answer using multiple pieces from the set.

An open-ended question should not aim to find one specific answer. Instead, the question should aim to focus on the journey towards a solution involving problem-solving skills and abilities. The animal spirits that possess the bones do not wish to babysit humans or hold their hands as they carry out complex tasks. The spirits are far more concerned with empowering people to solve their own problems with proactive solutions. You must keep this in mind when writing your questions, allowing for an answer with room for growth and development of the self. For example, you can ask the bones, 'where is my relationship going?' instead of 'how long will my relationship last?'. The first question can include many aspects of the relationship, such as its strengths, weaknesses, and dynamics. However, the second question has no room for introspection into the relationship.

You should try to be as specific as possible in your questioning. You should use names, places, times, and dates. These details can hook the spirits' attention and persuade them to offer you an equally detailed answer. You can also ask the bones follow-up clarifying questions after they have provided you with answers.

Highly personal questions are the most appropriate for bone-casting. Use questions that you may not want other people to know or hear. Reveal your inner turmoil and struggles to the spirits of the bones. They will appreciate your honesty and self-sacrifice in exposing yourself. Do not use the bones to answer questions that could just as quickly be answered elsewhere. For example, do not waste the spirit's time by asking how you can help your community. Instead, go directly to the community members and leaders and ask them what you can do. Instead, you should look at questions such as 'how can I combat the extreme jealousy I feel regarding my partner?' which is extremely sensitive, personal, and transparent.

Coming up with well-worded questions that can provide open-ended answers is a skill that you will come to develop through practice. Don't be discouraged if you have difficulty expressing yourself as intended during your first few bone-casting sessions. It's normal if you struggle to come up with good questions or not read and interpret the answers provided by the bones. The spirits do not expect practitioners to be highly skilled readers at the beginning of their bone-casting journey. They may even choose to make the process more difficult for you to test or allow room for you to prove yourself.

NINE

Using Your Own Bone Set

Let's begin to look into some of the various ways that casting bones are used. In a previous chapter, you were introduced to some of the important features to include in your bone set, with the most important piece being the one that represents yourself.

Primary Bones

These bones make up the core of a bone casting set and represent some of the significant elements of life. Most castings will incorporate all of these bones to provide a fuller and more comprehensive answer. These bones represent the main actors in your life. The ones that play active roles and influence your decision-making processes.

These bones include pieces to represent:

- Yourself, or if you are going to carry out bone casting ceremonies for others, you will need a bit to represent them
- The spirit world

- Your home
- Your health—You can further split up health into different categories such as mental health and physical health, or even more specific such as digestive health, fitness, etc
- Your partner and other key friends and family members
- Your community or tribe
- Your career, which could also incorporate financial aspects

Secondary Bones

The secondary bones are like the stage on which the primary bones perform. They provide additional context and descriptions of the primary bones.

Some important secondary pieces to consider adding to your collection include the following:

Yes and No

You can use separate pieces for each response or use two-sided bones with one side representing 'yes' and the other side representing 'no.'

Direction

Bones that can be used to identify basic directions, such as left, right, up and down, or north, south, east, and west. These can be individual pieces to represent each direction or multifaceted pieces where different faces represent different directions.

Good and Bad

Pieces that can be used to reveal good and bad energy, intentions, or actions. Again, you can use two separate pieces or a two-sided bone.

Human Emotions

Assign emotions such as happiness, sadness, and anger, to their own bones in the set.

Human Conditions
Bones to represent depression, anxiety, and other mental conditions.
Honesty and Deceit
Bones that can indicate whether a person is lying or being truthful.
Start and Finish
Beginning and end, or birth and death.
The Past, the Present, and the Future
Passive and Active
Bones that can be used to indicate whether actions should be taken or if you should be passive and continue waiting.

Personalized Meanings

You can always use bones in your own unique way as there are no set standards or rules associated with bone casting. You can use the bones in time-honored and traditional methods, such as the sangomas. Still, you can also use them in novel and unconventional ways. You can create entirely new systems that are utterly unique to you or use existing systems as a framework or a starting point. For example, if you have a particular passion or interest in astrology but are drawn strongly to the bones, you can assign astrological meanings to your bones:

The Sun
In traditional astrology, the Sun represents the self and the ego, which transposes well onto a bone-casting setup.
The Moon
The Moon is used to represent feelings and emotions.
Mercury
Mercury is the planet of intelligence, communication, understanding, and learning.
Venus
This planet represents love, beauty, and passion. This

would be an excellent way to represent a loved one using your bones.

Mars

Mars is the planet of war, fire, and desire.

Jupiter

This planet represents abundance, hope, and opportunity.

Saturn

This planet represents hard work, determination, discipline, and commitment.

Neptune

Neptune represents spiritual awareness and intuition.

Uranus

This planet represents individuality and transformation.

Pluto

This planet represents desire and power.

Tarot cards provide a comprehensive and strong framework of meanings and symbolism to incorporate into a bone casting set. There are two types of cards within a tarot deck. The Major Arcana and the Minor Arcana. The Major Arcana are the most popularized element of tarot, with twenty-two cards, each numbered from 0 to 21. Each major arcana represents an important step in life, following the development of a person's soul using societal archetypes. Each tarot card has a forward and reverses direction; if the card is pulled upside down, it is considered reversed. Reverse meanings are the opposite of the forward meaning.

00 - The Fool

The arcana representing birth, naivety, and innocence.

01 - The Magician

The arcana representing taking action.

02 - The High Priestess

The arcana representing awareness.

03 - The Empress

The arcana representing abundance.

04 - The Emperor
The arcana representing authority and power.
05 - The Hierophant
The arcana representing intellectual development.
06 - The Lovers
The arcana representing relationships and making choices.
07 - The Chariot
The arcana representing achievement and victory through effort.
08 - Strength
The arcana representing one's strengths, talents, and perseverance.
09 - The Hermit
The arcana representing introspection.
10 - Wheel of Fortune
The arcana representing destiny or fate.
11 - Justice
The arcana representing a decision-point and justice.
12 - The Hanged Man
The arcana representing self-sacrifice.
13 - Death
The arcana representing transitions and change.
14 - Temperance
The arcana representing balance and moderation
15 - The Devil
The arcana representing materialism and physical pleasures.
16 - The Tower
The arcana representing a crisis or sudden awakening.
17 - The Star
The arcana representing hope and inspiration.
18 - The Moon
The arcana representing deception and insecurity.
19 - The Sun

The arcana representing the self and life force.

20 - Judgement

The arcana representing redemption and reincarnation.

21 - The World

The arcana representing liberation, accomplishment, and peace.

Tarot cards hold highly detailed and specific meanings. They are instrumental in helping you to identify avenues of your own life that you wish to include in a bone casting set.

Throwing Your Bones

Many different methods and techniques are used to throw bones during a bone casting ceremony. Including mixing up and randomizing the bones, which hands you use to cast, and how the configurations are read and interpreted.

You can use bone-casting to answer a specific question or series of questions you pose to the bones and their animal spirits. You can also carry out unprompted bone casting where you do not have a question in mind. Both of these methods are valid approaches to communicating with the spirit world. However, it may become more difficult to read and interpret the bones without a clear question in mind. Instead of attempting to answer questions, the animal spirits will instead guide you to different aspects and avenues of life that they believe are important and deserving of more attention.

To begin a casting ceremony, it is customary in many cultures to start with simple introductions. Introduce yourself to the spirits, or introduce your clients to the spirits. Explain to them who you are and why you have come. If you do not have a highly specific reason, you can explain this. The ceremony space can be decorated in any way you see fit, whether darkening the windows to allow a little light in as possible or setting up crystals and sun catchers. You can burn incense and herbs appropriate to your cultural heritage and your intended practice, and you can also play music.

Before you begin asking the bones any questions, take some time to sit quietly and peacefully. Center your mind and do a simple meditation as you examine how your body feels as you sit in the space. Breathing exercises are also highly recommended to calm the mind and the body. This will help create a harmonious practice space where the spirits can safely enter into and interact.

Randomizing Your Bones

At the start of a bone-casting ceremony, you will need to ensure that your bones are mixed up thoroughly. If you store your bones in a drawstring bag or a box, you can use your hands to wade through the bones and mix them up gently. It is the tradition in some cultures to shake the bones, as the sangomas do. You can also choose to shake your bones in a bag, box, or basket. Be very careful not to be too rigorous, or you may damage some bones.

To shake the basket, you can move it back and forth, from side to side, or in a circular motion. Each motion will have an effect on how the bones are mixed. Depending on the purpose of the bone-casting, you can choose to use a particular shaking style, such as shaking in a circular motion in a clockwise direction, to incorporate additional energy into the bones. If a person comes for bone casting to help them with a difficult period in their life, you may choose to shake the bones back and forth to represent the removal of blockages. Carry out a bone casting for yourself to help you improve your spiritual abilities. You can use a clockwise motion to elevate the basket to represent the ongoing journey of constant learning and development. If a person comes for bone casting to deal with interpersonal issues, a side-to-side shake is suitable as it represents the relationships between people.

You can also choose to mix and randomize your bones using either your left hand, right hand, or a combination of both. Left-handedness and right-handedness hold different meanings in some cultures. For example, in Western Esotericism, the right and left hands represent the dichotomy between light and dark magic. The 'right-hand path' is concerned with white magic, benevolent magic, and the 'left-hand path' is associated with black magic and the occult. You can incorporate such beliefs into your own practice. When dealing with ancestral spirits and positive affirmations, mix the bones with your right hand. When dealing with demons, banishings, or negativity, you could mix the bones up using your left hand.

Casting

You can choose to cast your bone in any way that feels right to you. You will need to use your intuition to thoroughly mix the bones and cast them onto a surface. There are some frameworks that you can use to base your own practice on.

The most basic method for casting bones is to pick up a handful, hover above the throwing surface, and then let go. The bones will fall straight down onto the surface, where you can then read the different patterns and configurations. You can choose to let go of the bones from different heights, either very close to the ground or from a greater distance. This could represent the level of connection you are looking for from the spirit world or how much importance a particular question holds compared to others.

You can also throw the bones, giving them a small amount of momentum. You can throw them forwards, backward, or sideways. You can use such methods to represent different elements in the casting. For example, if you are casting to gain insight into a past event, throw the bones in a slightly backward direction to help represent the past.

Divination with Osteomancy

There are also methods that you can use without picking up the bones and casting them. For bone casting sets stored in soft fabric or animal hide bags, there are many ways to mix up the bones. Still, the most common casting method involves simply turning the bag upside down and letting the bones fall out naturally.

Reading the Bones

Reading the bones incorporates all of the knowledge you have gained during your practices. It is a holistic process that requires keen attention to detail and seeing the bigger picture. You can use many prescribed methods at the beginning of your bone casting journey, which you can choose to continue using or alter to better suit your needs. The following techniques will describe some of the methods that you can use to read bones when casting them onto a blank surface:

The Left to Right Method

All written languages are read in a particular direction, whether it is from left to right, right to left, or top to bottom. Bones can be read in the same way. This method is relatively easy to use. The first step in using this method is to identify the bone representing yourself or your client if you are performing a reading for someone else. Identify where the 'self' bone is in respect to the rest of the set; is it located in the center or near an edge, near the bottom, or the middle. Then identify which bones are touching the self bone, if any. These will be important for later. Then you can begin interpreting the bones from left to right.

Here is an example of a bone configuration that was cast after asking the question 'How can I improve my relationship with my friends and family?' I cast some bones for this reading, and the 'self' bone lands near the bottom-right edge; I will make a note of this. Then I will identify which bones are touching the 'self' bone. The bone representing loyalty and the future are both touching the 'self' bone in this example. Now the bones can be read from left to right. In this example, the bones are arranged from left to right as follows:

A Wishbone

Representing good luck.

A Femur Bone

Representing strength.

A Coin with Heads Facing Upwards

This represents a 'yes' answer.

A Sharp Curved Bone

Representing protection.

A Claw

Representing loyalty - is touching the self bone.

The Self Bone

Facing upwards.

A Tooth Marked with Notches on the Apex

Represents the future.

Broken Piece of Unknown Bone

Representing uncertainty.

Keeping the question in the forefront of your mind at all times, you can begin interpreting these bones by reading them from left to right. The 'self' has been identified, and it is touching two bones, one representing the future and one representing loyalty. This message could be interpreted to infer that the self is surrounded by loyal people and will continue to stay loyal into the future. Now consider these bones in the context of the rest of the casting. The first bone in the casting is a wishbone; this is a great omen that positively influences your relationships with others. The next bone represents strength, but it is not touching anything. This could be interpreted to highlight the strength of many relationships and the strength of yourself as an independent person. A coin with the 'yes' side facing upwards can confirm the previous interpretations. Moving more to the right, there is a bone representing protection. It sits close to the self bone but does not touch it. This can indicate that strong relationships can protect you from harm and protect those relationships themselves from harm. Next in the sequence is the self bone and its two partners. Finally, on the right-most side of the casting, there is a piece of unknown and broken bone which is a good representation of the unknown. This can be interpreted to mean that the animal spirits cannot be too sure about the future of the relationships.

Now that you have read each bone by itself, you can incorporate all of the information into one cohesive message. For example, the spirits in this casting shine a light on the many good relationships you have in your life and how you are surrounded by many loyal to you. However, there is uncertainty in the future, and the spirits cannot be sure of how long these relationships will last. To preserve the relationships for as long as possible, take action to protect yourself, and nurture your relationships more.

Distance Method

This is another method used to read bones with a plain throwing surface. In this method, when the bones are cast, their proximity to the reader or to the client is considered and incorporated into the reading. Objects and bones that land closer are deemed to be more imminent and important. In contrast, objects that land further away are only meant to add context. For example, suppose one of the bones lands right by the client's feet during a casting while others fall within the circle. In that case, this bone is clearly significant and should be featured prominently in the interpretations.

Similarly, sometimes a bone will be shot far into a corner of the room when casting. It may seem like a coincidence or accident, but there is no such thing. This bone is trying to communicate a pressing and urgent matter.

The 4 Directions Method

This method is meant to be used along with a marked throwing surface. The throwing surface, be it cloth or hide or a mat, must be marked with a large X, a cartesian plane (a central vertical line and a central horizontal line that cross each other in the center), or a medicine wheel. This leaves four different sections on the throwing surface. As mentioned previously, it is common to associate each of these sections with a cardinal direction, classical element, or even the seasons.

For example, if we carry out casting using a medicine wheel surface, we will have four quadrants representing north, east, west, and south. Each is associated with its own meanings. In the Ojibwe Tribe of North America, the north represents mental aspects. The east represents spiritual aspects, the south represents emotional aspects, and the west represents the physical aspects of one's life. A question such as 'what lessons am I supposed to learn from my breakup?' is a good and specific question that the spirits can work with. The bones are cast, and the 'self' bone happens to land right in the center of the medicine wheel. In many Native American cultures, this center point represents balance, a key aspiration. A claw used to convey anger and a black stone to represent bad luck fall into the west section. A femur bone representing the passage of time falls into the east section, a white shell representing purity, and a sunflower seed symbolizing virility falls into the south section. A rib bone representing protection falls into the north section. None of the bones touch each other.

These bones can be interpreted as follows; since the 'self' bone fell into the center, it highlights the need to balance life. Perhaps the failed relationships were not balanced. The 'anger' and 'bad luck' bones fell into the west section, representing the physical body. This could mean that the failed relationship was filled with too much anger and bad luck. Which has led to physical problems in the body, such as stiffness, inflammation, and chronic pain from tension. The femur bone can be interpreted to mean that the person's spirit has grown and developed throughout the relationship, which is a positive outcome obtained through struggle. The objects representing purity and virility fall into the emotional section of the medicine wheel. This can be interpreted to mean that the person felt unclean, unwanted, unproductive, and sterile in the relationship.

Now you need to use your knowledge of your bones, the medicine wheel, your own interpretations, and the client to create a holistic reading. For example, this reading shows that the past relationship likely failed due to an imbalance of power and emotion. Too many negative emotions plaguing everyday life to the point that they caused physical harm. The person should seek out a physical or a massage therapist to help them relieve tension from their body. However, the person did gain more spiritual enlightenment during the relationship. Likely due to their patience and willingness to work through problems. The medicine wheel and the bones show that this person needs to find someone more aligned with them and their values, especially in terms of purity and virility. Perhaps the person desperately wanted children, but their partner opposed them. The bones are trying to highlight the importance of clear communication at the beginning of a relationship and set down your expectations with your partner before running into deal-breaking problems.

Concentric Circles

One of the final methods for interpreting bones that will be discussed is the concentric circle method. Using a throwing surface that is decorated with concentric circles, usually no more than three, the bones are cast. Bones that land within the innermost circle are the most important and direct influences to consider. The second concentric circle is for less pressing issues. The outermost circle is for indirect influences.

Scrying

Scrying is a divination method used in many different ways by many different cultures. In the context of bone-casting, scrying refers to the reading and interpretation of bones as a whole picture rather than of many smaller and individual elements. For example, a bone caster uses a particular set of rib bones from a snake. Each rib bone looks very similar to the others. It is difficult to tell them apart without taking a closer look at the carefully inscribed symbols. Suppose a practitioner uses these bones in a casting ceremony. In that case, they will look at the bones as a whole, trying to determine any patterns visible in the configuration. For example, do the bones lie in a similar direction, or are they highly randomized? Do the bones cross over each other? Do they create any images?

Sequential Casting

Sequential casting is used when you need to ask the spirits multiple questions. All bones are collected and recast when a new question is posed in some practices, but only a few bones are cast per each question in other methods. This will depend on how many pieces you have in your set; more pieces will allow you to ask more questions without resetting everything.

Single-Bone Casting

Bone casting can also be carried out using only a single bone. Many types of bones are suited to this type of application, such as those with many sides or faces. Knucklebones, scapula, and skulls make for good bones in single-casting practices. These bones must have meanings assigned to each of their faces to work effectively. It is best to use this type of method for simple questions such as 'yes' or 'no' questions because the bones cannot provide more detail and context. This method is similar to using dice or flipping a coin.

Personalized Interpretations

In many divination practices, such as tarot, it is common for people to invent their own methods to read the cards. The same can be done with bone casting. You can choose any steps in the process. For example, you can choose to ask your spirits a question and then cast out three bones before asking another question and then selecting only one bone to cast. You can cast all of your bones simultaneously; you can create different groupings of bones that you cast at different times. You can also choose to cast your bones onto many different surfaces instead of just one. It is personalized, so the choice is ultimately yours.

Conclusion

This has been a comprehensive guide into the world of bone casting. This practice is undoubtedly one of the oldest forms of divination on Earth. It is strongly connected with animal spirits and ancestral spirits. You should now have all of the knowledge and expertise required to begin your journey to becoming a practitioner.

An experienced practitioner does not rush their processes and can sit back and receive messages from the universe without being prompted. As you progress through your journey to becoming a bone-caster, you will continue to learn and develop. Your intuition will evolve into a keen sense, and you will be able to interpret your bones just as if they spoke your language. Take your time, and be willing to put in the hard work required to build a solid foundation of wisdom. Always seek more knowledge.

The purpose of divination is to improve the world for the living. Use these magical tools wisely and responsibly, and do not attempt to take advantage of the power. The spirit world will find a way to retaliate against you. Use your bones to help yourself lead a happier and more fulfilling life. Use them to serve your community and aid in people's worries and trou-

Conclusion

bles; use them to protect the environment and prolong the survival of humans on Earth.

This book has covered many topics, which you can go back and refer to at any time. The complex and diverse history of the practice spans many continents. It has evolved and developed into a diverse array of rituals and traditions. You, too, can create your own unique practice that stems from ancient practice.

Your pathway forward is entirely up to you. Every aspect of your practice should reflect your personality, intentions, and desires. Every bone and object that you cast must be carefully selected, revered, and treated with respect. Every movement of your hand must be considered, and every direction that bones can fall must be accounted for. Always try to create a holistic and comprehensive picture when doing bone castings. Consider all of the information provided to you by your clients that come to seek help and combine this with your own knowledge.

Your perspective of the world, both the physical and the spiritual, is unique and unlike anyone else's. This is exactly as the gods intended. You offer an insight that nobody else can offer. Your interpretations and readings express your own soul that you can take with you when you enter the spirit world.

References

Abimbọla,W. (1997). Ifá : an exposition of Ifá literary corpus. Athelia Henrietta Press.

Andrew, G. R., & Park, G. K. (2001, February 16). Divination. Encyclopedia Britannica. https://www.britannica.com/topic/divination

Barron, A. (2019, November 14). Your "Palo Santo-Burning" Habit Is Causing The Deforestation Of What Indigenous Communities Consider A Sacred Tree. We Are Mitú. https://wearemitu.com/wearemitu/culture/your-palo-santo-burning-habit-is-causing-the-deforestation-of-what-indigenous-communities-consider-a-sacred-tree

Bascom, W. R. (1991). Ifa divination : communication between gods and men in West Africa. Indiana University Press.

Bindrik. (2019, May 16). The 30 Pieces You Need to Begin Bone Throwing Divination. Bindrik. https://bindrik.com/the-30-pieces-you-need-to-begin-bone-throwing-divination

Bones Shells And Curios. (2020, October 24). Bones, Shells, and Curios - Bone divination, bone reading, bone casting, conjure bones. Bones, Shells, and Curios.

References

https://bonesshellsandcurios.com/reading-surfaces-for-bone-divination/

Britton. (2016, May 27). Bone Reading Intro & Starting Guide. Archaic Honey. https://archaichoney.com/blog/2016/5/1/bone-reading-intro-starting-guide

Chat, W. (1998, May 5). Witchcraft - Wicca - Pagan - Druid - Witch. Wicca-Chat. http://www.wiccachat.com/circle.htm

Coles, D. (2017, May 29). Magical cleansing basics: How to get started. Spiral Nature Magazine. https://www.spiralnature.com/magick/magical-cleansing-basics/

Cosgrove, A. (2015, March 11). Ngombo Ya Kusekula (Divination Basket). ÌMỌ̀ DÁRA. https://www.imodara.com/discover/angola-chokwe-ngombo-ya-kusekula-divination-basket/

Croucamp, A. (2013). Traditional African Divination Systems As Information Technology. Mindburst Workshop. https://mindburstwork.com/sites/default/files/Traditional%20African%20divination%20systems%20as%20information%20technology_0.pdf

Dervenis, K. (2013). Oracle Bones Divination: The Greek I Ching. Simon and Schuster. https://books.google.co.za/books?hl=en&lr=&id=qF8oDwAAQBAJ&oi=fnd&pg=PT6&dq=bone+casting+divination&ots=SdS_k0OBV-&sig=4vUaj84EVQKyUXq4WieS3IcQb8#v=onepage&q=bone%20casting%20divination&f=false

Drummond, K. (2018, September 9). Grounding and Clearing And How It Can Help You. About Play. https://aboutplaytherapy.com/grounding-and-clearing-and-how-it-can-help-you

Eaton, A. (2019, December). Smoke Cleansing 101: How To Cleanse Your Home or Office with Plants and Herbs. Oui We. https://www.ouiwegirl.com/beauty/2019/12/4/smudg-

References

ing-101-how-to-cleanse-your-home-or-office-with-sage-palo-santo-and-sacred-plants

Eiselen, W. M. (2011). The Art of Divination As Practice By The Bamasemola. Bantu Studies, 6(1), 1–30. https://doi.org/DOI: 10.1080/02561751.1932.9676270

Estrada, J. (2020, January 20). I'm a Tarot Reader, and I Hate Getting These 8 Questions. Well+Good. https://www.wellandgood.com/questions-to-ask-in-tarot-readings/

Fisher, B. J. (2012). Exploring worldviews: A framework. TEACH Journal of Christian Education, 6(11), 50–56. https://doi.org/

Giraldus, C. (2004). The Journey Through Wales and the Description of Wales by Gerald of Wales. Penguin.

Grace, S. (2018, September 16). What are good vs. bad questions for divination? Medium. https://medium.com/@simonegrace/what-are-good-vs-bad-questions-for-divination-3bfb7069480e

Gruben, M. (2015, June 8). Intuitive vs. inductive divination: Which are you using? Grove and Grotto. https://www.groveandgrotto.com/blogs/articles/31321857-intuitive-vs-inductive-divination-which-are-you-using

Hart, A. (2017a, May 18). Throwing The Bones: How To Make And Use A Bone Set. The Traveling Witch. https://thetravelingwitch.com/blog/2018/5/14/throwing-the-bones-how-to-make-and-use-a-bone-set

Hart, A. (2017b, November 21). How To Cleanse: The Ultimate Guide For New Witches. The Traveling Witch. https://thetravelingwitch.com/blog/2017/11/21/how-to-cleanse-the-ultimate-guide-for-new-witches

Janzen, J. (1992). Ngoma: Discourses of Healing in Central and Southern Africa. Publishing.cdlib.org; University of California Press. http://www.jstor.org/stable/10.1525/j.ctt1pph77

References

Karade, I. (2020). The handbook of Yoruba religious concepts. Weiser Books.

Makgopa, M., & Koma, M. (2009). The use of ditaola (divination bones) among indigenous healers in Sekhukhune District, Limpopo Province: indigenous African healing practices. Indilinga African Journal of Indigenous Knowledge Systems, 8(1), 51–58. https://www.researchgate.net/profile/Mokgale-Makgopa-2/publication/315083739_The_Use_Of_Ditaola_Divination_Bones_Among_Indigenous_Healers_In_Sekhukhune_District_Limpopo_Province/links/5ed935d092851c9c5e7c620c/The-Use-Of-Ditaola-Divination-Bones-Among-Indigenous-Healers-In-Sekhukhune-District-Limpopo-Province.pdf

Mark, E. (2016, February 26). Oracle Bones. World History Encyclopedia. https://www.worldhistory.org/Oracle_Bones/

Mccoy, D. (2016). The Viking spirit : an introduction to Norse mythology and religion. Createspace Independent Publishing Platform.

Mikanowski, J. (2016, September 28). How to Read the Bones Like a Scapulimancer. JSTOR Daily. https://daily.jstor.org/how-to-read-bones-like-a-scapulimancer/

Mutwa, C. V. (1999). Indaba, my children. Grove Press.

Mutwa, C. V., & Larsen, S. (2003). Zulu shaman : dreams, prophecies, and mysteries. Destiny Books.

Nassner, A. (2018, October 17). Cleansing 101: Keeping your home's energy in check. Curbed. https://archive.curbed.com/2018/10/17/17951378/crystals-cleansing-pink-salt-smudging-how-to

Otherworldly Oracle. (2020, January 8). Throwing Bones: How to Make and Read Your Own Osteomancy Set. Otherworldly Oracle. https://otherworldlyoracle.com/throwing-bones-osteomancy/

Peterson, W. H. and D. (2015, October 2). The casting of

References

lots in ancient Israel. Deseret News. https://www.deseret.com/2015/10/2/20573546/the-casting-of-lots-in-ancient-israel

Pit, R. (2018, April 22). Bone Magick: Or Using Bones, Fangs, Feathers, Claws, and Shells in Animal Magick and Ancestor Work. Nettle's Garden - the Old Craft. https://www.theoldcraft.com/2018/04/22/bone-magick-or-using-bones-fangs-feathers-claws-and-shells-in-animal-magick-and-ancestor-work/

Restaurant, G. (2015, March 31). What It Means to "Throw The Bones" in African Culture. GOLD Restaurant. https://goldrestaurant.co.za/african-culture-and-tradition/what-it-means-to-throw-the-bones-in-african-culture/

Rojas, A. (2016). Reading maize: A narrative and psychological approach to the study of divination in Mesoamerica. Journal for the Study of Religions and Ideologies, 15(1), 102–124.

Ross, W. (2021, February 5). Throwing the Bones. Spirituality & Health. https://www.spiritualityhealth.com/articles/2021/02/05/throwing-the-bones

SABC Digital News. (2020a, March 25). Top 5 Credo Mutwa quotes. SABC News. https://www.sabcnews.com/sabcnews/top-5-credo-mutwa-quotes/

SABC Digital News. (2020b, March 25). Top 5 Credo Mutwa quotes. SABC News. https://www.sabcnews.com/sabcnews/top-5-credo-mutwa-quotes/

Scott. (2021, March 1). Scottish Folk magic and the dead (part three)–folk charms, herbs for the dead and second sight. Cailleach's Herbarium. https://cailleachs-herbarium.com/2017/10/scottish-folk-magic-and-the-dead-part-three-folk-charms-herbs-for-the-dead-and-second-sight/

Sebastian, A. (2018, June). Cleansing & Purification, pt 3: What's the Difference? Althaea Sebastiani. https://www.ladyalthaea.com/every-day-is-magickal/cleansing-purification-pt-3-whats-the-difference

References

Sebastiani, A. (2017, August 26). What is Throwing the Bones? Lady Althaea. https://www.ladyalthaea.com/everyday-is-magickal/what-is-throwing-the-bones

Shi, D. B. (2016). North Asian magic : spellcraft from Manchuria, Mongolia, and Siberia. The Yronwode Institution For The Preservation And Popularization Of Indigenous Ethnomagicology (Yippie.

South African History Online. (2011). Indigenous medicine and traditional healing. In www.sahistory.org.za. Grade 6 - Term 4: Medicine through time. https://www.sahistory.org.za/article/indigenous-medicine-and-traditional-healing

South African History Online. (2013, December 4). Vusamazulu Credo Mutwa. South African History Online. https://www.sahistory.org.za/people/vusamazulu-credo-mutwa

Tennant, H. (2020, November 23). How to Clean Animal Bones for Display. Empress of Dirt; Melissa, J. Will. https://empressofdirt.net/how-clean-animal-bones/

The Bible Answer. (2017, April 18). What did it mean to Cast Lots in the Bible? The Bible Answer. https://thebibleanswer.org/cast-lots-bible-divination/

Tyler, D. (2016, March 7). Your Guide to Rune Divination. Rune Divination. https://runedivination.com/your-guide-to-rune-divination/

UNESCO. (2014). Mongolian knuckle-bone shooting. Intangible Cultural Heritage, United Nations Educational, Scientific and Cultural Organization. https://ich.unesco.org/en/RL/mongolian-knuckle-bone-shooting-00959

van Binsbergen, W. (1996). Southern African divination: connections in space and time. Journal of Religion in Africa, 26(1), 2–29. http://www.quest-journal.net/shikanda/african_religion/trans.htm

Wigington, P. (2019, September 29). Using Animal Bones for Divination and Magic. Learn Religions. https://www.learnreligions.com/bone-divination-2562499

References

Wigington, P. (2020, January). What Is Rune Casting? Origins and Techniques. Learn Religions. https://www.learnreligions.com/rune-casting-4783609

wikiHow Staff. (2020, April 28). How to Clean Bones. WikiHow. https://www.wikihow.com/Clean-Bones

Wikimedia Contributors. (2020, September 23). Cleromancy. In Wikipedia, the Free Encyclopedia. https://en.wikipedia.org/wiki/Cleromancy

Wikimedia Contributors. (2021a, June 5). Oracle bone. In Wikipedia, the Free Encyclopedia. https://en.wikipedia.org/wiki/Oracle_bone#:~:text=Oracle%20bones%20(Chinese%3A%20%E7%94%B2%E9%AA%A8%3B

Wikimedia Contributors. (2021b, June 19). Methods of divination. In Wikipedia, the Free Encyclopedia. https://en.wikipedia.org/wiki/Methods_of_divination

Wikipedia Contributors. (2021, June 15). Shagai. In Wikipedia, the Free Encyclopedia; https://en.wikipedia.org/wiki/Shagai

Wikipedia contributors. (2021a, April 19). Knucklebones. In Wikipedia, the Free Encyclopedia. https://en.wikipedia.org/w/index.php?title=Knucklebones&oldid=1018743213

Wikipedia contributors. (2021b, May 13). Vusamazulu Credo Mutwa. In Wikipedia, the Free Encyclopedia. https://en.wikipedia.org/w/index.php?title=Vusamazulu_Credo_Mutwa&oldid=1022936122

Wikipedia contributors. (2021c, May 13). Vusamazulu Credo Mutwa. In Wikipedia, the Free Encyclopedia. https://en.wikipedia.org/w/index.php?title=Vusamazulu_Credo_Mutwa&oldid=1022936122

Wikipedia contributors. (2021d, June 19). Runes. In Wikipedia, the Free Encyclopedia. https://en.wikipedia.org/w/index.php?title=Runes&oldid=1029345329

Willow. (2019a, March 30). Bone Magic Series: Bones and Skulls: How to Use Them in Magic. Flying the Hedge.

References

https://www.flyingthehedge.com/2019/03/bone-magic-series-bones-and-skulls-how.html

Willow, A. (2019b, September 27). Bone Magic Series: Feeding Your Bones. Flying the Hedge. https://www.flyingthehedge.com/2019/09/bone-magic-series-feeding-your-bones.html

Wood, F. E. (2017). Objects and Immortals: The Life of Obi in Ifa-Orişa Religion. Doctoral dissertation, Harvard University, Graduate School of Arts & Sciences. http://nrs.harvard.edu/urn-3:HUL.InstRepos:41140237

About the Author

Monique Joiner Siedlak is a writer, witch, and warrior on a mission to awaken people to their greatest potential through the power of storytelling infused with mysticism, modern paganism, and new age spirituality. At the young age of 12, she began rigorously studying the fascinating philosophy of Wicca. By the time she was 20, she was self-initiated into the craft, and hasn't looked back ever since. To this day, she has authored over 40 books pertaining to the magick and mysteries of life.

To find out more about Monique Joiner Siedlak artistically, spiritually, and personally, feel free to visit her **official website**.

www.mojosiedlak.com

facebook.com/mojosiedlak
twitter.com/mojosiedlak
instagram.com/mojosiedlak
pinterest.com/mojosiedlak
bookbub.com/authors/monique-joiner-siedlak

More Books by Monique

African Spirituality Beliefs and Practices
Hoodoo
Seven African Powers: The Orishas
Cooking for the Orishas
Lucumi: The Ways of Santeria
Voodoo of Louisiana
Haitian Vodou
Orishas of Trinidad
Connecting With Your Ancestors
Black Magic
The Orishas
Vodun: West Africa's Spiritual Life

Practical Magick
Wiccan Basics
Candle Magick
Wiccan Spells
Love Spells
Abundance Spells
Herb Magick

Moon Magick
Creating Your Own Spells
Gypsy Magic
Protection Magick
Celtic Magick

Spiritual Growth and Personal Development
Creative Visualization
Astral Projection for Beginners
Meditation for Beginners
Reiki for Beginners
Manifesting With the Law of Attraction
Being an Empath Today

Get a Handle on Life
Stress Management
Get a Handle on Anxiety
Get a Handle on Depression
Get a Handle on Procrastination

The Yoga Collective
Yoga for Beginners
Yoga for Stress
Yoga for Back Pain
Yoga for Weight Loss
Yoga for Flexibility
Yoga for Advanced Beginners
Yoga for Fitness
Yoga for Runners
Yoga for Energy
Yoga for Your Sex Life
Yoga to Beat Depression and Anxiety
Yoga for Menstruation
Yoga to Detox Your Body

More Books by Monique

Yoga to Tone Your Body

A Natural Beautiful You
Creating Your Own Body Butter
Creating Your Own Body Scrub
Creating Your Own Body Spray

Last Chance Join My Newsletter!

If you missed it, I have a free gift available for you and wanted to remind you it's still available.

mojosiedlak.com/newsletter-signup

Thank you for reading my book.
I really appreciate all your feedback and would love to hear what you have to say! Please leave your review at your favorite retailer!

Thank you

Printed in Great Britain
by Amazon